CHOOSING GOD INSTEAD OF THE WORLD

CHOOSING GOD INSTEAD OF THE WORLD: LEARNING FROM THE LIVES OF JACOB AND JOSEPH

Photo source:
unsplash.com

Recipe source:
Ester, LGG Swahili Branch

Information and data source:
Joshua Project, joshuaproject.net/languages/swh, accessed February 2022.

Bibliography:
Ross, Allen P. *Creation and Blessing: A Guide to the Study and Exposition of the Book of Genesis*. Grand Rapids, Michigan: Baker Book House, 1998.

Published in the United States of America, Library of Congress Catalogue-in-Publication data, Printed in USA.

978-1-7365811-8-6

27 26 25 24 23 22

6 5 4 3 2 1

WHEN WOMEN ARE
EQUIPPED WITH THE
KNOWLEDGE OF GOD'S
TRUTH, THE WORLD
IS TRANSFORMED ONE
WOMAN AT A TIME.

JOURNAL BELONGS TO

DATE

\ \

CONTENTS

You

HAVE BEEN PRAYED FOR; IT IS NOT A COINCIDENCE YOU ARE PARTICIPATING IN THIS STUDY.

WELCOME FRIEND!

We are glad you have decided to join us in this Bible study! You have been prayed for; it is not a coincidence you are participating in this study.

Our prayer for you is simple: that you will grow closer to our Lord as you dig into His Word each and every day. Each day before you read the assigned passage, pray and ask God to help you understand it. Invite Him to speak to you through His Word. Then listen. Believe He will be faithful to speak to you, and be faithful to listen and obey.

Take time to read the verses over and over again. The Bible tells us that if we seek wisdom like silver, and search for it like hidden treasure, then we will understand how to fear the Lord, and we will discover knowledge about God (Prov 2:4-5).

All of us here at Love God Greatly can't wait for you to get started, and we hope to see you at the finish line. Endure, persevere, press on; don't give up! Finish well what you are beginning today.

We will be here every step of the way, cheering for you! We are in this together. Be expectant that God has much in store for you in this study. Journey with us as we learn to love God greatly with our lives!

WE NEED EACH OTHER, AND WE LIVE LIFE BETTER TOGETHER. WOULD YOU CONSIDER REACHING OUT AND DOING THIS STUDY WITH SOMEONE?

Love God Greatly exists to inspire, encourage, and equip women around the world to love God greatly with their lives.

INSPIRE women to make God's Word a priority in their daily lives through Bible study resources.

ENCOURAGE women in their walks with God through online community and personal accountability.

EQUIP women to grow in their faith so they can effectively reach others for Christ.

We start with a simple Bible reading plan, but it doesn't stop there. Some women gather in homes and churches locally, while others connect online with women across the globe, Whatever the method, we lovingly lock arms and unite for this purpose: to love God greatly with our lives.

At Love God Greatly, you'll find real, authentic women. You'll find women who desire less of each other, and a whole lot more of Jesus. Women who long to know God through His Word because we believe that truth transforms and sets us free. Women who are better together, saturated in God's Word and in community with one another.

Love God Greatly is committed to providing quality Bible study materials and believes finances should never get in the way of a woman being able to participate in one of our studies. All journals are available to download for free from LoveGodGreatly.com.

Our journals and books are also available for sale on Amazon. Search for "Love God Greatly" to see all of our Bible study journals and books.

YOU'LL FIND WOMEN WHO ARE IMPERFECT, YET FORGIVEN.

Love God Greatly is a 501 (C)(3) non-profit organization. Funding for Love God Greatly comes through donations and proceeds from our online Bible study journals and books.

One-hundred percent of proceeds go directly back into supporting Love God Greatly and helping us inspire, encourage, and equip women all over the world with God's Word.

Arm-in-arm and hand-in-hand, let's do this together.

OUR MISSION

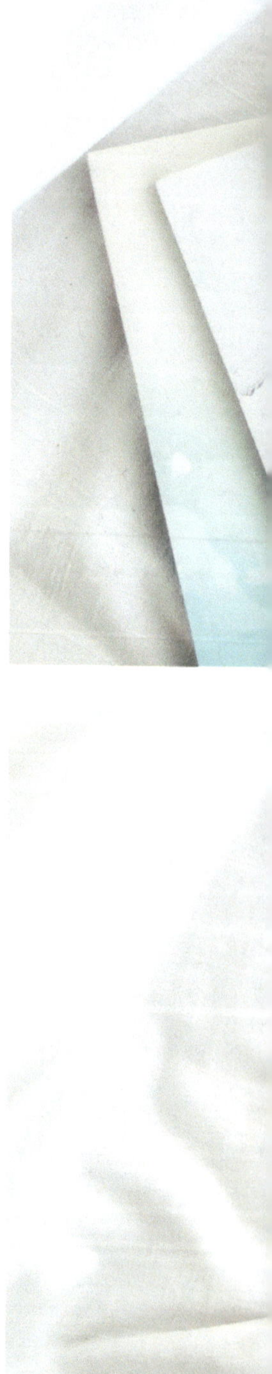

THE NEED

Billions of women around the world don't have access to God's Word in their native language. Those who do, don't have access to women's Bible studies designed and written with them in mind.

THE MISSION

At Love God Greatly, we create Bible studies in 40+ languages. We equip missionaries, ministries, local churches, and women with God's Word at an unprecedented rate by allowing our journals to be downloaded from our international sites at no cost.

Through studying the Bible in their own language with like-minded communities, women are trained and equipped with God's Word.

We believe when women read and apply God's Word to their lives and embrace His unchanging love for them, the world is a better place. We know one woman in God's Word can change a family, a community, and a nation... one woman at a time.

PARTNER WITH US

We would love for you to join us in our mission of giving women all over the world access to God's Word and quality Bible study resources! For any questions or for more information, email us or visit us online. We would love to hear from you!

INFO@LOVEGODGREATLY.COM

LOVEGODGREATLY.COM

AT LOVE GOD GREATLY,
WE CREATE BIBLE STUDIES
IN 40+ LANGUAGES.

SOAP

Bible Study Method

At Love God Greatly, we believe that the Word of God is living and active. The words of Scripture are powerful and effective and relevant for life in all times and all cultures. In order to interpret the Bible correctly, we need an understanding of the context and culture of the original writings.

As we study the Bible, we use the SOAP Bible Study Method. The acronym stands for Scripture, Observation, Application, and Prayer. It's one thing simply to read Scripture. When you interact with it, intentionally slowing down to reflect, truths start jumping off the page. The SOAP Method allows us to dig deeper into Scripture and see more than we would if we simply read the verses. It allows us not only to be hearers of the Word, but doers as well (James 1:22).

YOU WILL NEVER WASTE TIME IN GOD'S WORD. IT IS LIVING, POWERFUL, AND EFFECTIVE, AND HE SPEAKS TO US THROUGH IT.

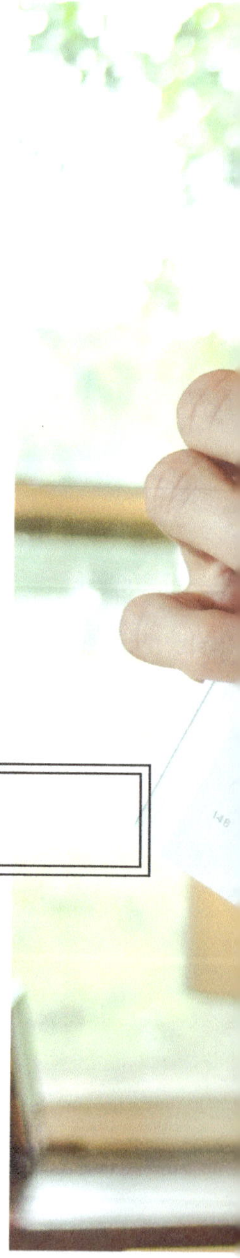

In this journal, we read a passage of Scripture and then apply the SOAP Method to specific verses. Using this method allows us to glean a greater understanding of Scripture, which allows us to apply it effectively to our lives.

The most important ingredients in the SOAP Method are your interaction with God's Word and your application of it to your life. Take time to study it carefully, discovering the truth of God's character and heart for the world.

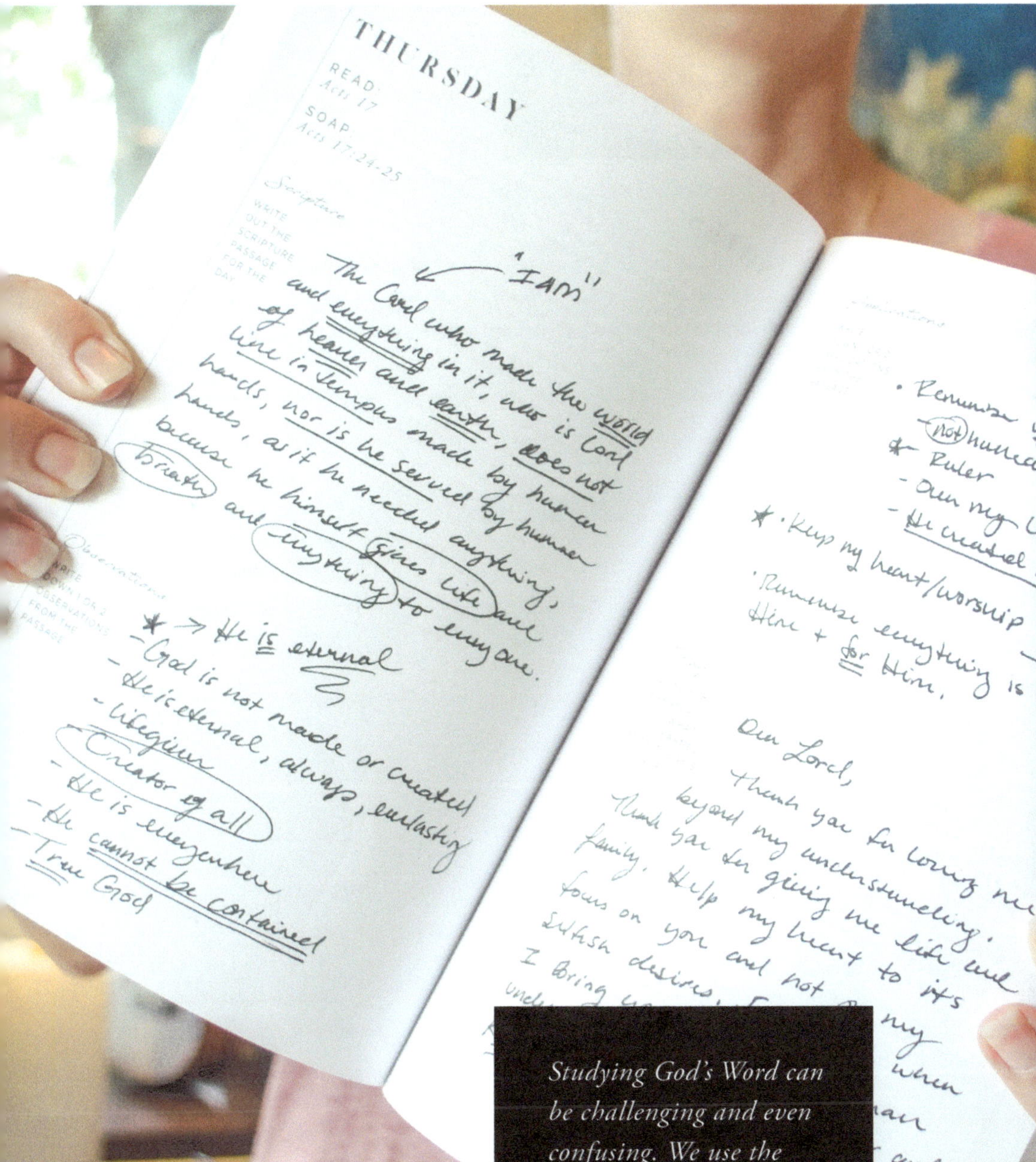

Studying God's Word can be challenging and even confusing. We use the SOAP method to help us simplify our study and focus on key passages.

SOAP
Bible Study Method

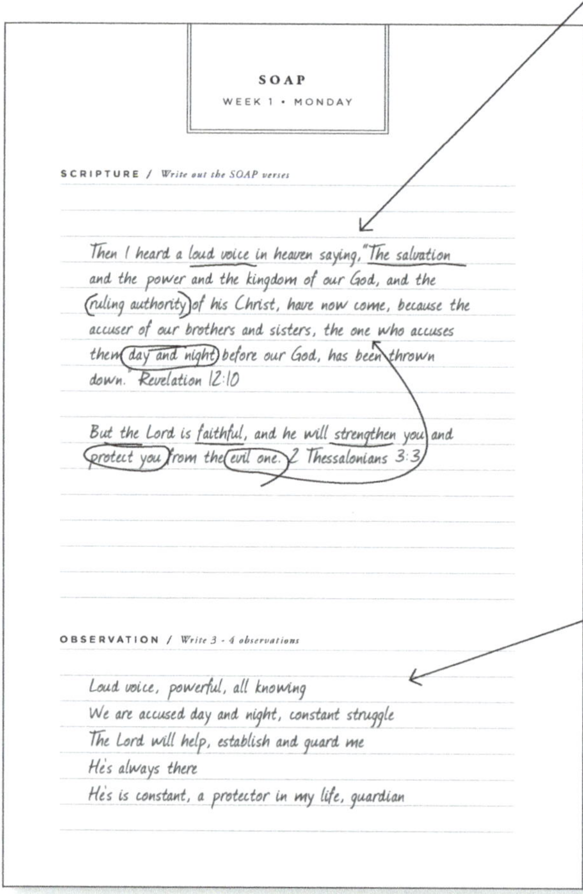

S
STANDS FOR SCRIPTURE

Physically write out the SOAP verses.

You'll be amazed at what God will reveal to you just by taking the time to slow down and write out what you are reading!

O
STANDS FOR OBSERVATION

What do you see in the verses that you're reading?

Who is the intended audience? Is there a repetition of words?

What words stand out to you?

A
STANDS FOR APPLICATION

This is when God's Word becomes personal.

What is God saying to you today? How can you apply what you just read to your own personal life?

What changes do you need to make? Is there action you need to take?

APPLICATION / *Write down 1 - 2 applications*

Remind myself of God's strength is more powerful than anything
Memorize these verses and say them daily this week
Ask God to strengthen my faith in Him
Trust God that he will deliver me from evil
Pray for my brothers and sister's in Christ

PRAYER / *Write out a prayer over what you learned*

Dear Lord,

Thank you for being constant, faithful, and loving towards me and my life. Help me to further my trust and faith in you daily and through difficult times.

Help me to know you're alway there by my side, guarding, and protecting me. Remind me of the suffering of others and to be able to help and encourage them in their growth.

I ask all these things in Jesus name.
Amen

P
STANDS FOR PRAYER

Pray God's Word back to Him.
Spend time thanking Him.

If He has revealed something to you during this time in His Word, pray about it.

If He has revealed some sin that is in your life, confess. And remember, He loves you dearly.

AWASI

LANGUAGE HIGHLIGHT

TESTIMONY

LGG Swahili Branch

I was born and raised in a Christian family, in a small village called Kinyinya in Tanzania. We were taught to go to church and give an offering, but I did not know why I was going to church.

While in high school, I met a friend who shared the gospel of Christ with me, and my life changed. I gave my life to Christ, and since then I have been walking in God's ways and serving Him. In 2006, I went back to college and, while there, served God as a secretary of an organization called Students' Christian Fellowship. Serving in that fellowship enabled me to grow more spiritually. We ministered to our fellow students, as well as the surrounding community, through service and evangelism. I also served as a translator during mid-week and Sunday church services.

While working with an international organization, I met a woman who told me about Love God Greatly and their ministry, translating Bible studies into different languages. I volunteered to translate these studies into Swahili. I served alone with no one on my team for about three years. I continued to ask God to keep giving me opportunities to serve Him and for others to help translate the materials.

God has brought five women to my team to help work on the Swahili materials. We all live in different countries, but we are a team. Through this ministry and serving God, I have been blessed with incredible friendships, and I have seen God provide for me and sustain me. Our branch continues to grow, and we currently have sixteen women studying the Bible together in the Swahili language.

GOD CONTINUES TO WORK IN MY LIFE, AND I HAVE SEEN HIM DO MIRACULOUS THINGS.

God continues to work in my life, and I have seen Him do miraculous things. He has provided a job for me after three years of being unemployed. He has blessed me with a community around the world and the opportunity to serve Him. I give all the glory and honor to Him alone.

"I was young, now I am old. I have never seen the godly abandoned, or their children forced to search for food" (Psalm 37:25).

Ester

LGG Swahili Branch

LANGUAGE	GLOBAL SPEAKERS	TO CONNECT WITH THIS BRANCH
Swahili	3,817,000	Facebook: LGG Swahili Instagram: @lggswahilibranch Email: lggswahilibranch@gmail.com

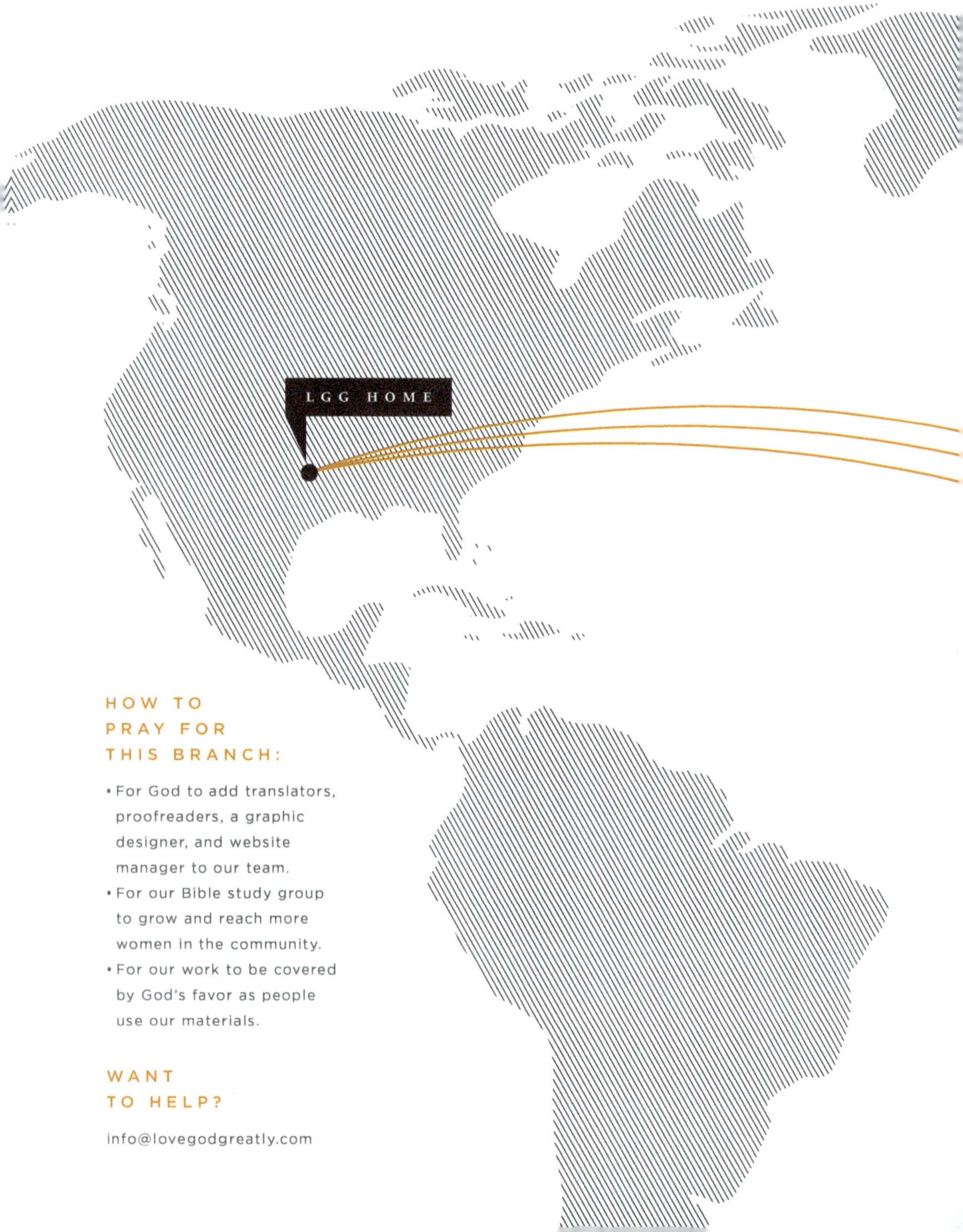

HOW TO PRAY FOR THIS BRANCH:

- For God to add translators, proofreaders, a graphic designer, and website manager to our team.
- For our Bible study group to grow and reach more women in the community.
- For our work to be covered by God's favor as people use our materials.

WANT TO HELP?

info@lovegodgreatly.com

LANGUAGE HIGHLIGHT

GLOBAL OUTREACH

LGG Swahili Branch

Do you know someone who could use our Love God Greatly Bible studies in the Swahili language?

If so, make sure to tell them all the amazing Bible study resources we provide to help equip them with God's Word!

LANGUAGE HIGHLIGHT

RECIPE

LGG Swahili Branch

Ndizi na Nyama

(MEAT AND BANANA STEW)

INGREDIENTS

2 CUPS OF KIDNEY BEANS

¾ POUND BEEF TOP SIRLOIN
cut into small cubes

12 GREEN BANANAS OR PLANTAINS

2 LARGE ONIONS

4 TOMATOES

2 LARGE EGGPLANTS

1 TBSP OF SALT

4 CUPS OF WATER

DIRECTIONS

Soak the kidney beans for 3 hours.

Cut the meat into small cubes, and cook it on a stove over medium heat. In another pan, boil the beans until they are almost fully-cooked. When both beans and meat are ready, add the beans to the pan with the meat and continue cooking.

Peel the bananas (or plantains) and cut them in half. Mix the bananas in with the beans and meat. Slice the onions, tomatoes, and eggplants and add to the mixture of beans, bananas, and meat, adding salt to taste. Add the water to the pan and cover it, cooking until the bananas are soft and well-cooked. Add more water until the desired consistency is reached for the soup.

Serve hot and enjoy!

KNOW THESE TRUTHS

GOD LOVES YOU

God's Word says, "For this is the way God loved the world: He gave his one and only Son, so that everyone who believes in him will not perish but have eternal life" (John 3:16).

OUR SIN SEPARATES US FROM GOD

We are all sinners by nature and by choice, and because of this we are separated from God, who is holy. God's Word says, "for all have sinned and fall short of the glory of God" (Rom 3:23).

JESUS DIED SO YOU MIGHT HAVE LIFE

The consequence of sin is death, but God's free gift of salvation is available to us. Jesus took the penalty for our sin when He died on the cross.

God's Word says, "For the payoff of sin is death, but the gift of God is eternal life in Christ Jesus our Lord" (Rom 6:23); "But God demonstrates his own love for us, in that while we were still sinners, Christ died for us" (Rom 5:8).

JESUS LIVES!

Death could not hold Him, and three days after His body was placed in the tomb Jesus rose again, defeating sin and death forever. He lives today in heaven and is preparing a place in eternity for all who believe in Him.

Jesus says, "There are many dwelling places in my Father's house. Otherwise, I would have told you, because I am going away to make ready a place for you. And if I go and make ready a place for you, I will come again and take you to be with me, so that where I am you may be too" (John 14:2–3).

KNOW YOU CAN BE FORGIVEN

Accepting Jesus as your Savior is not about what you can do, but rather about having faith in what Jesus has already done. It takes recognizing that you are a sinner, believing that Jesus died for your sins, and asking for forgiveness by placing your full trust in Jesus' work on the cross on your behalf.

God's Word says, "if you confess with your mouth that Jesus is Lord and believe in your heart that God raised him from the dead, you will be saved. For with the heart one believes and thus has righteousness and with the mouth one confesses and thus has salvation" (Rom 10:9–10).

ACCEPT CHRIST'S FREE GIFT OF SALVATION

Practically, what does that look like? With a sincere heart, you can pray a simple prayer like this:

Jesus,
I know that I am a sinner. I don't want to live another day without embracing the love and forgiveness that You have for me. I ask for Your forgiveness. I believe that You died for my sins and rose from the dead. I surrender all that I am and ask You to be Lord of my life. Help me to turn from my sin and follow You. Teach me what it means to walk in freedom as I live under Your grace, and help me to grow in Your ways as I seek to know You more. Amen.

CONNECT AND GROW

If you just prayed this prayer (or something similar in your own words) we'd love to connect with you!

You can email us at info@lovegodgreatly.com. We'd love to celebrate with you, pray with you, and help you connect to a local church. We are here to encourage you as you begin your new life as a child of God.

Let's Begin

CHOOSING GOD INSTEAD OF THE WORLD

ONE CUP

Introduction

We are constantly making choices. Often, our choices involve choosing the things of the world or choosing the things of God. We can easily be tempted to choose what is easy, what allows us to get ahead quickly, or what we believe is best. The lives of Jacob and Joseph show us how God disciplines His children when they choose the things of the world and how He blesses them when they choose, instead, to follow Him.

The Book of Genesis is a combination of two narratives. Chapters 1–11 record God's creation of the world and the beginnings of humankind, sin, grace, redemption, and promise. Chapters 12–50 chronicle the lives of the patriarchs of God's chosen nation: Abraham, Isaac, Jacob, and Joseph. God chose this family to be the one through whom He would send His Messiah into the world, the One who would save the world from sin and death.

Most biblical scholars agree that Genesis was written by Moses during the time the Israelites wandered in the Desert of Zin, around 1440 B.C. The lives of the patriarchs were recorded by Moses for the generation of Israelites who would enter the land God had promised to give them. As they prepared to enter the Promised Land of Canaan, the words of Genesis reminded them who their God was and why a life committed to Him was worth pursuing.

This Bible study focuses on the lives of Jacob and Joseph, beginning in Genesis chapter 25. As we study these men's lives, we will discover the faithfulness of God to His chosen people through promise, blessing, discipline, suffering, persecution, famine, testing, reconciliation, and restoration. Jacob and his family were constantly faced with decisions to follow God's ways or to follow the ways of the world. While they were not perfect, God continued to work in their lives to bring about His plans for them. God Himself was the hero, continually molding and shaping His people as He prepared them for the future.

GOD IS ALWAYS FAITHFUL TO HIS PEOPLE, HIS PROMISES, AND HIS COVENANT.

We can learn to love God greatly by studying His promise-keeping character. In this study, we will see what it means to walk in obedience, and we will see the faithfulness of God to discipline His people and bring them back to Him when they sin. God is always faithful to His people, His promises, and His covenant. May we be open to learning all He has in store for us, expectant that He will reveal Himself to us in new ways as we seek to know Him through His Word.

In addition to this study, check out *In the Beginning* and *Faith over Perfection* for a full study of the Book of Genesis!

READING PLAN

WEEK 1

○ *Monday*
Read: Genesis 25:19–26; Isaiah 43:1
SOAP: Isaiah 43:1

○ *Tuesday*
Read: Genesis 25:27–34; 1 John 2:15–17
SOAP: 1 John 2:15–17

○ *Wednesday*
Read: Genesis 26:34—28:9; Romans 9:6–18
SOAP: Genesis 28:3–4

○ *Thursday*
Read: Genesis 28:10–22
SOAP: Genesis 28:15

○ *Friday*
Read: Genesis 29:1–30; Galatians 6:6–10; Hebrews 12:6
SOAP: Galatians 6:7–9

WEEK 2

○ *Monday*
Read: Genesis 29:31—30:24; Colossians 3:1–3
SOAP: Colossians 3:1–3

○ *Tuesday*
Read: Genesis 30:25–43; Proverbs 3:1–12
SOAP: Proverbs 3:9–10

○ *Wednesday*
Read: Genesis 31; 1 John 3:18–24
SOAP: 1 John 3:23–24

○ *Thursday*
Read: Genesis 32:1–21; Psalm 56:3–4, 10–11
SOAP: Psalm 56:3–4

○ *Friday*
Read: Genesis 32:22–32
SOAP: Genesis 32:28

WEEK 3

○ *Monday*
Read: Genesis 33; 2 Corinthians 5:16–21
SOAP: 2 Corinthians 5:18–19

○ *Tuesday*
Read: Genesis 34; Romans 12:17–21
SOAP: Romans 12:19

○ *Wednesday*
Read: Genesis 35; Deuteronomy 30:15–20
SOAP: Deuteronomy 30:15–16

○ *Thursday*
Read: Genesis 36:1—37:1; Genesis 27:28–29, 39–40;

; Luke 16:10

26; 2 Corinthians 4:7–18
4:17–18

th 4:12; Matthew 1:2–16

nes 1:2–18
3, 17

alm 13

1–52

READING PLAN

WEEK 5

- *Monday*
  Read: Genesis 42; 2 Corinthians 7:9–10
  SOAP: 2 Corinthians 7:9–10
- *Tuesday*
  Read: Genesis 43; 1 Peter 3:8–9
  SOAP: 1 Peter 3:8–9
- *Wednesday*
  Read: Genesis 44; John 15:12–13; 1 John 1:8—2:2
  SOAP: John 15:12–13
- *Thursday*
  Read: Genesis 45:1–15
  SOAP: Genesis 45:5
- *Friday*
  Read: Genesis 45:16—46:30
  SOAP: Genesis 46:2–4

WEEK 6

- *Monday*
  Read: Genesis 46:31—47:27; Proverbs 8:12–17
  SOAP: Proverbs 8:15–17
- *Tuesday*
  Read: Genesis 47:28—48:22; Isaiah 55:8–9; Philippians 1:6; Hebrews 11:13, 21
  SOAP: Hebrews 11:13, 21
- *Wednesday*
  Read: Genesis 49:1–28; Psalm 139:1–6, 16
  SOAP: Psalm 139:16
- *Thursday*
  Read: Genesis 49:29—50:26; Exodus 13:19; John 14:1–3
  SOAP: John 14:1–3
- *Friday*
  Read: Genesis 1:31; 3:4–6; 6:5–8; 18:22–25; 50:19–20
  SOAP: Genesis 50:19–20

YOUR GOALS

Write three goals you would like to focus on as you begin each day and dig into God's Word. Make sure you refer back to these goals throughout the next weeks to help you stay focused. You can do it!

ONE

TWO

THREE

"I am with you!
I will protect you
wherever you go
and will bring
you back to this
land. I will not
leave you until
I have done what
I promised you."

Genesis 28:15

PRAY

Write down your prayer requests and praises for this week.

WEEKLY CHALLENGE

God made a covenant with Abram, giving him a great promise. This week, read Genesis 15 and note the promise God made to Abram and his descendants. How do you see God fulfilling His promise to Abram's descendants through Jacob in this week's reading?

WEEK 1
Monday

READ

Genesis 25:19–26

This is the account of Isaac, the son of Abraham. Abraham became the father of Isaac. 20 When Isaac was forty years old, he married Rebekah, the daughter of Bethuel the Aramean from Paddan Aram and sister of Laban the Aramean. 21 Isaac prayed to the Lord on behalf of his wife because she was childless. The Lord answered his prayer, and his wife Rebekah became pregnant. 22 But the children struggled inside her, and she said, "Why is this happening to me?" So she asked the Lord, 23 and the Lord said to her, "Two nations are in your womb, and two peoples will be separated from within you. One people will be stronger than the other, and the older will serve the younger." 24 When the time came for Rebekah to give birth, there were twins in her womb. 25 The first came out reddish all over, like a hairy garment, so they named him Esau. 26 When his brother came out with his hand clutching Esau's heel, they named him Jacob. Isaac was sixty years old when they were born.

Isaiah 43:1

Now, this is what the Lord says, the one who created you, O Jacob, and formed you, O Israel: "Don't be afraid, for I will protect you. I call you by name, you are mine.

SOAP

WEEK 1 • MONDAY

SOAP / *Isaiah 43:1*

SCRIPTURE / *Write out the SOAP verses*

25:21 Issac prayed to the Lord on behalf of his wife
because she was childless. The Lord answered
his prayer and Rebekah became pregnant
25:22 The children struggled inside her and she
said "Why is this happening to me" so she
asked the Lord.
25:23 And the Lord said to her "Two nations are
in your womb, and two peoples will be
seperated from within you. One people will
be stronger than the other, and the older
will serve the younger".
25:26 When his brother came out with his
hand clutching Esau's they named him
Jacob. Issac was 60 yr. old when they
were born

OBSERVATION / *Write 3 - 4 observations*

- Issac prayed to the Lord on behalf of his wife
- The Lord answered Issac's prayer and Rebekah became pregnant
- The children were struggled inside the womb
- The Lord said to Rebekah "Two nations are in your womb.

APPLICATION / *Write down 1 - 2 applications*

25:21 The Lord hears our prayers
25:22 Sometimes things happen and we have no understanding of why
25:23 The Lords message may not be clear but he has a purpose in everything that he does

- devote time to the Lord
- Talk to him, Ask for answers to things I don't understand

PRAYER / *Write out a prayer over what you learned*

- Oh Lord please teach me your word
- Help me to understand your word
- help me to read your word every day
- Help me to be a better person as through your word.

Amen

DEVOTIONAL

WEEK 1 • MONDAY

SOAP

Isaiah 43:1

Now, this is what the LORD says, the one who created you, O Jacob, and formed you, O Israel: "Don't be afraid, for I will protect you. I called you by name, you are mine."

INTO THE TEXT

The Book of Genesis provides us with an account of the creation of the earth and God's plan for redemption. Sin entered the world (Genesis 3), bringing many consequences for humankind. God promised to redeem the world from sin and its effects by sending a deliverer, one who would destroy the enemy and the curse of sin once and for all.

God used a family to bring His Son, Jesus, into the world to provide redemption for humanity. That family began with a man named Abram (later named Abraham). God promised to make Abram into a great nation, to give his descendants a land of their own, and to bless the world through his family. While Abram did not see these promises fully fulfilled in his lifetime, God continued to work out His purposes through Abram's descendants. In this study, we'll focus on the life of Jacob, Abraham's grandson, and his family. Even though Jacob was not the firstborn, God chose him to be the one through whom He would fulfill His promises.

Jacob's story begins in the womb, as he struggled with his brother, Esau. When Jacob was born, he was clutching Esau's heel. He was named Jacob, a word similar to a Hebrew word meaning "to seize the heel, to trip up, to deceive." Jacob literally seized Esau's heel at birth and he was known for the way he figuratively seized the heels of others through deception for much of his life. As we study the life of Jacob, we'll see all the ways he deceived others for personal gain, both out of selfishness and fear.

God knew everything Jacob would do in his life, and He still chose him to be the heir to His great promise. God knew Jacob would be a deceiver. God knew he would waver in his faith and often choose the things of the world over the things of God. God also knew that Jacob would exercise great faith, that he would worship and follow Him, and that he would be the father of God's chosen nation.

God chose an imperfect man, known for deception, and fulfilled His great promise for the world through his family. As the events of Jacob's life unfold throughout our study, we are reminded of this truth: God always keeps His promises. He knows us intimately, formed us entirely, and loves us deeply. God desires our obedience and our faith, but nothing can thwart His purposes or keep Him from fulfilling His promises.

WEEK 1
Tuesday

READ

Genesis 25:27–34

When the boys grew up, Esau became a skilled hunter, a man of the open fields, but Jacob was an even-tempered man, living in tents. 28 Isaac loved Esau because he had a taste for fresh game, but Rebekah loved Jacob. 29 Now Jacob cooked some stew, and when Esau came in from the open fields, he was famished. 30 So Esau said to Jacob, "Feed me some of the red stuff—yes, this red stuff—because I'm starving!" (That is why he was also called Edom.) 31 But Jacob replied, "First sell me your birthright." 32 "Look," said Esau, "I'm about to die! What use is the birthright to me?" 33 But Jacob said, "Swear an oath to me now." So Esau swore an oath to him and sold his birthright to Jacob. 34 Then Jacob gave Esau some bread and lentil stew; Esau ate and drank, then got up and went out. So Esau despised his birthright.

1 John 2:15–17

Do not love the world or the things in the world. If anyone loves the world, the love of the Father is not in him, 16 because all that is in the world (the desire of the flesh and the desire of the eyes and the arrogance produced by material possessions) is not from the Father, but is from the world. 17 And the world is passing away with all its desires, but the person who does the will of God remains forever.

SOAP

WEEK 1 • TUESDAY

SOAP / *1 John 2:15–17*

SCRIPTURE / *Write out the SOAP verses*

25:28 Issac loved Esau because he had a taste for fresh game but Rebekah love Jacob.

25:30 So Esau said to Jacob "feed me some of the red stuff - yes this red stuff because I'm starving"

25:31 But Jacob replied "first sell me your birth right"

25:32 Look said Esau "I'm about to die, what use is a birthright to me?"

25:33 But Jacob said "swear to me now"

25:34 Then Jacob gave Esau some bread and lentil stew, Esau ate and drank then got up and went out

OBSERVATION / *Write 3 - 4 observations*

25:30 Esau 'demanded' that Jacob give him food because he was starving

25:31 But Jacob replied "first sell me your birthright"

- Jacob didnt give Esau food out of the kindness of his heart or brotherly love
- Esau was willing to give up something so precious as his birthright in exchange for something else.

APPLICATION / *Write down 1 - 2 applications*

PRAYER / *Write out a prayer over what you learned*

DEVOTIONAL

WEEK 1 • TUESDAY

SOAP

1 John 2:15–17

Do not love the world or the things in the world. If anyone loves the world, the love of the Father is not in him, because all that is in the world (the desire of the flesh and the desire of the eyes and the arrogance produced by material possessions) is not from the Father, but is from the world. And the world is passing away with all its desires, but the person who does the will of God remains forever.

INTO THE TEXT

In the exchange between Jacob and Esau over the birthright, we find no lasting resolution between the brothers and no divine approval for either of their actions. However, the inclusion of the story sets up several important plot lines: the contrast between Jacob and Esau, the conflict between the brothers, and the beginnings of the fulfillment of God's promise for the older to serve the younger.

Esau is described as a profane person who despised the things of God and sought a life of worldly freedom. Jacob so desperately desired the blessing of God that he would go to any means to acquire it. Esau was wild, Jacob was calm. Esau was physical, Jacob was shrewd. Esau was loved by Isaac and Jacob was loved by Rebekah. While Jacob sought to acquire God's blessings, Esau sought to fulfill his fleshly desires. Both were skilled hunters, Esau with wild game and Jacob in craftiness.

Neither Jacob's nor Esau's actions in this story were exemplary. Esau allowed his flesh, his desire to satisfy his physical hunger, to take ultimate importance, even over the sacred things of God. He lived to satisfy his flesh and acted on impulse, causing him to despise his birthright. Though it is clear Jacob manipulated and controlled his brother to get what he wanted, the text does not make moral judgments on Jacob's actions the way it does on Esau's. God used this event to carry out His plan to elevate Jacob to supremacy over his brother, as He had promised.

As the events of Jacob's life unfold in Genesis, we will see the importance of choosing between God's way and the way of the world or of personal gain. Jacob was continually faced with choices between God's best and his own way. As followers of Christ, we are called to live differently from the world. We cannot live like Esau did, seeking to satisfy our flesh. Instead, we are to seek the things of God. However, even when we highly esteem God's blessing the way Jacob did, we are not excused from sin. We must still act in accordance with God's law, being honest and upright, even if deception is the easier option. The world is passing away, but when we do the will of God we find eternal life.

WEEK 1

Wednesday

READ

Genesis 26:34—28:9

When Esau was forty years old, he married Judith the daughter of Beeri the Hittite, as well as Basemath the daughter of Elon the Hittite. 35 They caused Isaac and Rebekah great anxiety. 27:1 When Isaac was old and his eyes were so weak that he was almost blind, he called his older son Esau and said to him, "My son!" "Here I am!" Esau replied. 2 Isaac said, "Since I am so old, I could die at any time. 3 Therefore, take your weapons—your quiver and your bow—and go out into the open fields and hunt down some wild game for me. 4 Then prepare for me some tasty food, the kind I love, and bring it to me. Then I will eat it so that I may bless you before I die." 5 Now Rebekah had been listening while Isaac spoke to his son Esau. When Esau went out to the open fields to hunt down some wild game and bring it back, 6 Rebekah said to her son Jacob, "Look, I overheard your father tell your brother Esau, 7 'Bring me some wild game and prepare for me some tasty food. Then I will eat it and bless you in the presence of the LORD before I die.' 8 Now then, my son, do exactly what I tell you! 9 Go to the flock and get me two of the best young goats. I'll prepare them in a tasty way for your father, just the way he loves them. 10 Then you will take it to your father. Thus he will eat it and bless you before he dies." 11 "But Esau my brother is a hairy man," Jacob protested to his mother Rebekah, "and I have smooth skin! 12 My father may touch me! Then he'll think I'm mocking him and I'll bring a curse on myself instead of a blessing." 13 So his mother told him, "Any curse against you will fall on me, my son! Just obey me! Go and get them for me!" 14 So he went and got the goats and brought them to

WEEK 1
Wednesday

Genesis 26:34—28:9 (continued)

his mother. She prepared some tasty food, just the way his father loved it. 15 Then Rebekah took her older son Esau's best clothes, which she had with her in the house, and put them on her younger son Jacob. 16 She put the skins of the young goats on his hands and the smooth part of his neck. 17 Then she handed the tasty food and the bread she had made to her son Jacob. 18 He went to his father and said, "My father!" Isaac replied, "Here I am. Which are you, my son?" 19 Jacob said to his father, "I am Esau, your firstborn. I've done as you told me. Now sit up and eat some of my wild game so that you can bless me." 20 But Isaac asked his son, "How in the world did you find it so quickly, my son?" "Because the Lord your God brought it to me," he replied. 21 Then Isaac said to Jacob, "Come closer so I can touch you, my son, and know for certain if you really are my son Esau." 22 So Jacob went over to his father Isaac, who felt him and said, "The voice is Jacob's, but the hands are Esau's." 23 He did not recognize him because his hands were hairy, like his brother Esau's hands. So Isaac blessed Jacob. 24 Then he asked, "Are you really my son Esau?" "I am," Jacob replied. 25 Isaac said, "Bring some of the wild game for me to eat, my son. Then I will bless you." So Jacob brought it to him, and he ate it. He also brought him wine, and Isaac drank. 26 Then his father Isaac said to him, "Come here and kiss me, my son." 27 So Jacob went over and kissed him. When Isaac caught the scent of his clothing, he blessed him, saying, "Yes, my son smells like the scent of an open field which the Lord has blessed. 28 May God give you the dew of the sky and the richness of the earth, and plenty of grain and new wine. 29 May peoples serve you and nations bow down to you. You will be lord over your brothers, and the sons of your mother will bow down to you. May those who curse you be

WEEK 1
Wednesday

26:34—28:9 (continued)

cursed, and those who bless you be blessed." 30 Isaac had just finished blessing Jacob, and Jacob had scarcely left his father's presence, when his brother Esau returned from the hunt. 31 He also prepared some tasty food and brought it to his father. Esau said to him, "My father, get up and eat some of your son's wild game. Then you can bless me." 32 His father Isaac asked, "Who are you?" "I am your firstborn son," he replied, "Esau!" 33 Isaac began to shake violently and asked, "Then who else hunted game and brought it to me? I ate all of it just before you arrived, and I blessed him. He will indeed be blessed!" 34 When Esau heard his father's words, he wailed loudly and bitterly. He said to his father, "Bless me too, my father!" 35 But Isaac replied, "Your brother came in here deceitfully and took away your blessing." 36 Esau exclaimed, "Jacob is the right name for him! He has tripped me up two times! He took away my birthright, and now, look, he has taken away my blessing!" Then he asked, "Have you not kept back a blessing for me?" 37 Isaac replied to Esau, "Look! I have made him lord over you. I have made all his relatives his servants and provided him with grain and new wine. What is left that I can do for you, my son?" 38 Esau said to his father, "Do you have only that one blessing, my father? Bless me too!" Then Esau wept loudly. 39 So his father Isaac said to him, "See here, your home will be by the richness of the earth, and by the dew of the sky above. 40 You will live by your sword but you will serve your brother. When you grow restless, you will tear off his yoke from your neck." 41 So Esau hated Jacob because of the blessing his father had given to his brother. Esau said privately, "The time of mourning for my father is near; then I will kill my brother Jacob!" 42 When Rebekah heard what her older son Esau had said, she quickly summoned her younger son Jacob

WEEK 1
Wednesday

26:34—28:9 (continued)

and told him, "Look, your brother Esau is planning to get
revenge by killing you. 43 Now then, my son, do what I
say. Run away immediately to my brother Laban in Haran.
44 Live with him for a little while until your brother's rage
subsides. 45 Stay there until your brother's anger against
you subsides and he forgets what you did to him. Then I'll
send someone to bring you back from there. Why should
I lose both of you in one day?" 46 Then Rebekah said to
Isaac, "I am deeply depressed because of the daughters of
Heth. If Jacob were to marry one of these daughters of
Heth who live in this land, I would want to die!" 28:1 So
Isaac called for Jacob and blessed him. Then he commanded
him, "You must not marry a Canaanite woman! 2 Leave
immediately for Paddan Aram! Go to the house of Bethuel,
your mother's father, and find yourself a wife there, among
the daughters of Laban, your mother's brother. 3 May the
Sovereign God bless you! May he make you fruitful and
give you a multitude of descendants! Then you will become
a large nation. 4 May he give you and your descendants
the blessing he gave to Abraham so that you may possess
the land God gave to Abraham, the land where you have
been living as a temporary resident." 5 So Isaac sent Jacob
on his way, and he went to Paddan Aram, to Laban son of
Bethuel the Aramean and brother of Rebekah, the mother
of Jacob and Esau. 6 Esau saw that Isaac had blessed Jacob
and sent him off to Paddan Aram to find a wife there. As he
blessed him, Isaac commanded him, "You must not marry
a Canaanite woman." 7 Jacob obeyed his father and mother
and left for Paddan Aram. 8 Then Esau realized that the
Canaanite women were displeasing to his father Isaac. 9
So Esau went to Ishmael and married Mahalath, the sister
of Nebaioth and daughter of Abraham's son Ishmael, along
with the wives he already had.

WEEK 1
Wednesday

Romans 9:6–18

It is not as though the word of God had failed. For not
all those who are descended from Israel are truly Israel,
7 nor are all the children Abraham's true descendants;
rather "***through Isaac will your descendants be counted***."
8 This means it is not the children of the flesh who are
the children of God; rather, the children of promise are
counted as descendants. 9 For this is what the promise
declared: "***About a year from now I will return and Sarah***
will have a son." 10 Not only that, but when Rebekah had
conceived children by one man, our ancestor Isaac— 11
even before they were born or had done anything good or
bad (so that God's purpose in election would stand, not by
works but by his calling)— 12 it was said to her, "***The older***
will serve the younger," 13 just as it is written: "***Jacob I***
loved, but Esau I hated." 14 What shall we say then? Is
there injustice with God? Absolutely not! 15 For he says
to Moses: "***I will have mercy on whom I have mercy, and***
I will have compassion on whom I have compassion." 16
So then, it does not depend on human desire or exertion,
but on God who shows mercy. 17 For the scripture says to
Pharaoh: "***For this very purpose I have raised you up, that***
I may demonstrate my power in you, and that my name
may be proclaimed in all the earth." 18 So then, God has
mercy on whom he chooses to have mercy, and he hardens
whom he chooses to harden.

SOAP

WEEK 1 • WEDNESDAY

SOAP / *Genesis 28:3–4*

SCRIPTURE / *Write out the SOAP verses*

OBSERVATION / *Write 3 - 4 observations*

APPLICATION / *Write down 1 - 2 applications*

PRAYER / *Write out a prayer over what you learned*

DEVOTIONAL

WEEK 1 • WEDNESDAY

SOAP

Genesis 28:3–4

"May the Sovereign God bless you! May he make you fruitful and give you a multitude of descendants! Then you will become a large nation. May he give you and your descendants the blessing he gave to Abraham so that you may possess the land God gave to Abraham, the land where you have been living as a temporary resident."

INTO THE TEXT

Even though God's commands are clear and His blessing abundant, we often create situations through deception and manipulation that destroy our relationships. Jacob's family's actions offer us a warning: regardless of what we think we deserve, it is always better to trust God's provision instead of trusting our plans.

God was clear in His choice to bless Jacob. Romans 9 explains how God chose to bless Jacob and not Esau, Isaac's firstborn. Instead of believing in God's promise and waiting for Him to act, Jacob trusted his plans and methods of receiving the blessing. He deceived his father and his brother and effectively shattered the family relationships.

God indeed had a plan to bless Jacob that didn't include a moral failure. Yet despite Jacob's sin, God blessed him. God allowed Jacob to obtain the blessing this way. Though God would later discipline Jacob, He showed him mercy by giving him the blessing. God is working in all aspects of our lives, even through our sin and disobedience. Even in our failure to trust Him, He can (and does) accomplish His purposes, but we may create unnecessary heartache and pain when we go our own way. When God makes a promise, He already has a plan to fulfill it.

As Isaac sent Jacob to Paddan Aram to find a wife, he reminded him of the promises God made to Abraham. God would make Jacob into a great nation, give him the land, and allow his descendants to be a blessing to all the people on the earth. God's promises had not been thwarted by poor decisions. His covenant promise to the family of Abraham would continue. Though there were always threats to the promise, God always came through. He was faithful to Abraham and faithful to Isaac. He would continue to be faithful to Jacob and his descendants in the future, fulfilling the covenant He made with Abraham.

Even though we sin, God can use us. He can turn our conflicts into blessings and bring peace to shattered relationships. He can redeem and work for good through any act of sin, no matter how grievous it is. He is in the business of restoration. He is in the business of using broken people. The Bible truthfully records even the failures of the "heroes of the faith" so that we can see the merciful character of God. He redeems, restores, and rebuilds even the most shattered of hearts, relationships, communities, and nations. We can trust Him.

WEEK 1
Thursday

READ

Genesis 28:10–22

Meanwhile Jacob left Beer Sheba and set out for Haran.
11 He reached a certain place where he decided to camp
because the sun had gone down. He took one of the stones
and placed it near his head. Then he fell asleep in that
place 12 and had a dream. He saw a stairway erected on
the earth with its top reaching to the heavens. The angels
of God were going up and coming down it 13 and the
LORD stood at its top. He said, "I am the LORD, the God
of your grandfather Abraham and the God of your father
Isaac. I will give you and your descendants the ground you
are lying on. 14 Your descendants will be like the dust of
the earth, and you will spread out to the west, east, north,
and south. And so all the families of the earth may receive
blessings through you and through your descendants. 15 I
am with you! I will protect you wherever you go and will
bring you back to this land. I will not leave you until I have
done what I promised you!" 16 Then Jacob woke up and
thought, "Surely the LORD is in this place, but I did not
realize it!" 17 He was afraid and said, "What an awesome
place this is! This is nothing else than the house of God!
This is the gate of heaven!" 18 Early in the morning Jacob
took the stone he had placed near his head and set it up
as a sacred stone. Then he poured oil on top of it. 19 He
called that place Bethel, although the former name of the
town was Luz. 20 Then Jacob made a vow, saying, "If God
is with me and protects me on this journey I am taking and
gives me food to eat and clothing to wear, 21 and I return
safely to my father's home, then the LORD will become my
God. 22 Then this stone that I have set up as a sacred stone
will be the house of God, and I will surely give you back a
tenth of everything you give me."

SOAP

WEEK 1 • THURSDAY

SOAP / *Genesis 28:15*

SCRIPTURE / *Write out the SOAP verses*

OBSERVATION / *Write 3 - 4 observations*

APPLICATION / *Write down 1 - 2 applications*

PRAYER / *Write out a prayer over what you learned*

DEVOTIONAL

WEEK 1 • THURSDAY

SOAP

Genesis 28:15

"I am with you! I will protect you wherever you go and will bring you back to this land. I will not leave you until I have done what I promised you."

INTO THE TEXT

Jacob had deceived his father and brother. Even though his father had blessed him too, Esau was still angry with Jacob. Jacob quickly became a fugitive because of his sin. As he set out on his journey, both to find a wife and escape his brother's wrath, his father's parting words confirmed God's blessing and promise.

As he traveled, Jacob reached a certain place and camped for the night. While the place seemed of no significance initially, it became a holy place for Jacob and his descendants. It was in this place that Jacob's journey of faith began.

God appeared to him in a dream, revealing Himself and His promises. God gave Jacob the same specific promise He had given to his father and grandfather: he would have many descendants, he would receive the land, and all the families of the earth would be blessed through him. God promised to be with Jacob, to protect him and never leave him.

As Jacob woke up, he recognized the divine encounter. He acknowledged God's presence and the holiness of the place. Jacob named the place Bethel. The place he rested was a town called Luz, but Jacob renamed it. Like many places involved in God's promise, this place was renamed because it marked a significant turning point in the fulfillment of the promise. It was here that the Lord became Jacob's God and Jacob vowed to worship Him.

Jacob's journey of faith was full of major turning points. Here, God's presence turned a fugitive into a worshiper. A man of deception became a man of faith (though he would wrestle with this sin for many years). It was not the last time Jacob would have a midnight encounter with God that would change his life. Jacob vowed to remember this moment and this place by marking the place with a stone.

God's presence filled the place where Jacob was. Jacob had done nothing to earn God's favor. God chose Jacob and continued to pursue him, and Jacob responded in worship. When we encounter God's presence through His Word, it should lead us to worship. We do not need to wait for a midnight encounter to experience God's presence. If we are followers of Christ, we can experience God's presence and the assurance of His promises every day through His Word and His Holy Spirit. He is with us as He was with Jacob. He has given us incredible promises in His Word. May we respond as Jacob did, with worship and commitment.

WEEK 1
Friday

READ

Genesis 29:1–30

So Jacob moved on and came to the land of the eastern people. 2 He saw in the field a well with three flocks of sheep lying beside it, because the flocks were watered from that well. Now a large stone covered the mouth of the well. 3 When all the flocks were gathered there, the shepherds would roll the stone off the mouth of the well and water the sheep. Then they would put the stone back in its place over the well's mouth. 4 Jacob asked them, "My brothers, where are you from?" They replied, "We're from Haran." 5 So he said to them, "Do you know Laban, the grandson of Nahor?" "We know him," they said. 6 "Is he well?" Jacob asked. They replied, "He is well. Now look, here comes his daughter Rachel with the sheep." 7 Then Jacob said, "Since it is still the middle of the day, it is not time for the flocks to be gathered. You should water the sheep and then go and let them graze some more." 8 "We can't," they said, "until all the flocks are gathered and the stone is rolled off the mouth of the well. Then we water the sheep." 9 While he was still speaking with them, Rachel arrived with her father's sheep, for she was tending them. 10 When Jacob saw Rachel, the daughter of his uncle Laban, and the sheep of his uncle Laban, he went over and rolled the stone off the mouth of the well and watered the sheep of his uncle Laban. 11 Then Jacob kissed Rachel and began to weep loudly. 12 When Jacob explained to Rachel that he was a relative of her father and the son of Rebekah, she ran and told her father. 13 When Laban heard this news about Jacob, his sister's son, he rushed out to meet him. He embraced him and kissed him and brought him to his house. Jacob told Laban how he was related to him. 14 Then Laban said to him, "You are

WEEK 1

Friday

Genesis 29:1–30 (continued)

indeed my own flesh and blood." So Jacob stayed with him
for a month. 15 Then Laban said to Jacob, "Should you
work for me for nothing because you are my relative? Tell
me what your wages should be." 16 (Now Laban had two
daughters; the older one was named Leah, and the younger
one Rachel. 17 Leah's eyes were tender, but Rachel had a
lovely figure and beautiful appearance.) 18 Since Jacob had
fallen in love with Rachel, he said, "I'll serve you seven
years in exchange for your younger daughter Rachel." 19
Laban replied, "I'd rather give her to you than to another
man. Stay with me." 20 So Jacob worked for seven years
to acquire Rachel. But they seemed like only a few days to
him because his love for her was so great. 21 Finally Jacob
said to Laban, "Give me my wife, for my time of service
is up. And I want to sleep with her." 22 So Laban invited
all the people of that place and prepared a feast. 23 In the
evening he brought his daughter Leah to Jacob, and he slept
with her. 24 (Laban gave his female servant Zilpah to his
daughter Leah to be her servant.) 25 In the morning Jacob
discovered it was Leah! So Jacob said to Laban, "What in
the world have you done to me? Didn't I work for you in
exchange for Rachel? Why have you tricked me?" 26 "It is
not our custom here," Laban replied, "to give the younger
daughter in marriage before the firstborn. 27 Complete my
older daughter's bridal week. Then we will give you the
younger one too, in exchange for seven more years of work."

WEEK 1
Friday

Genesis 29:1–30 (continued)

28 Jacob did as Laban said. When Jacob completed Leah's
bridal week, Laban gave him his daughter Rachel to be
his wife. 29 (Laban gave his female servant Bilhah to his
daughter Rachel to be her servant.) 30 Jacob slept with
Rachel as well. He also loved Rachel more than Leah.
Then he worked for Laban for seven more years.

Galatians 6:6–10

Now the one who receives instruction in the word must
share all good things with the one who teaches it. 7 Do
not be deceived. God will not be made a fool. For a
person will reap what he sows, 8 because the person who
sows to his own flesh will reap corruption from the flesh,
but the one who sows to the Spirit will reap eternal life
from the Spirit. 9 So we must not grow weary in doing
good, for in due time we will reap, if we do not give up.
10 So then, whenever we have an opportunity, let us do
good to all people, and especially to those who belong to
the family of faith.

Hebrews 12:6

"***For the Lord disciplines the one he loves and chastises every son he accepts.***"

SOAP

WEEK 1 • FRIDAY

SOAP / *Galatians 6:7–9*

SCRIPTURE / *Write out the SOAP verses*

OBSERVATION / *Write 3 - 4 observations*

APPLICATION / *Write down 1 - 2 applications*

PRAYER / *Write out a prayer over what you learned*

DEVOTIONAL

WEEK 1 • FRIDAY

SOAP

Galatians 6:7–9

Do not be deceived. God will not be made a fool. For a person will reap what he sows, because the person who sows to his own flesh will reap corruption from the flesh, but the one who sows to the Spirit will reap eternal life from the Spirit. So we must not grow weary in doing good, for in due time we will reap, if we do not give up.

INTO THE TEXT

After Jacob's dream at Bethel, he continued on his journey. He came to a well that had been covered to regulate the distribution of water to nearby flocks. As he spoke with the shepherds he discovered they knew his uncle, Laban, and that his daughter was coming to that very well with her sheep. Jacob recognized the divine providence of God as Rachel, the daughter of his mother's brother, arrived at the same well.

God was working mightily in Jacob's life. When Rachel arrived with her sheep, Jacob removed the stone that was covering the well so her sheep could drink. The blessing of God in Jacob's life led him to do great acts of service for others. He was confident in God's direction and it led him to bless those around him.

As Jacob stayed with Laban, he fell in love with Rachel. In exchange for marrying her, Jacob vowed to work for Laban for seven years. Yet, when the time came for Rachel to be given to Jacob, the deceiver was deceived. Laban gave Leah, his firstborn daughter, to Jacob instead of Rachel. Though he was able to marry Rachel soon after, Jacob was made to work another seven years for his second bride.

Jacob reaped what he had sown. Jacob had deceived his father and brother, and now he had been deceived. Jacob was not the firstborn, yet he had stolen the blessing of the firstborn. Laban deceived Jacob in giving him his firstborn daughter. The similarities are no coincidence; Laban's dishonesty to Jacob was used by God to discipline Jacob for his sin of deception.

God was still working mightily in Jacob's life. As the encounter at the well was a blessing, so also was this discipline. Instead of leaving Jacob to his sin, God intervened and disciplined him to remove sin from his life. The discipline Jacob received did not negate God's promise; it solidified it. For Jacob to receive the blessings of the promise, he would also be disciplined as a child of God.

God's blessing in our lives is two-fold: divine encounters and divine discipline. When God shows us our sin and allows us to repent, it is indeed a blessing. While it may not always feel pleasant or comfortable, God's discipline is a gift. May we continue to sow in the Spirit, and accept the discipline of our loving heavenly Father as we reap a harvest for His kingdom.

REFLECT

WEEK 1

1. *Why is our faith important to God? Why is obedience to God's commands important? How are the two related?*

2. *What does it mean to choose the things of God? Can you choose the things of God and the things of the world? Why or why not?*

3. *Do you believe God will provide for you without your help? In what ways do you depend on your own strength or cleverness instead of depending on God?*

4. *How do you respond when God intervenes in your life? Are you led to worship like Jacob was, or do you tend to explain His work as mere coincidence?*

5. *Have you experienced times when God has clearly disciplined you? Do you view God's discipline as a blessing?*

JOURNAL

your thoughts

JOURNAL

your thoughts

Therefore, if you have been raised with Christ, keep seeking the things above, where Christ is, seated at the right hand of God. Keep thinking about things above, not things on earth, for you have died and your life is hidden with Christ in God.

Colossians 3:1–3

PRAY

Write down your prayer requests and praises for this week.

WEEKLY CHALLENGE

This week, record the major events of Jacob's life. Do these things occur because of Jacob's plans or God's deliverance? How does Jacob's manipulation or impatience affect each outcome? Take time to reflect on the ways you attempt to "help" God accomplish His purposes.

WEEK 2
Monday

READ

Genesis 29:31–30:24

When the Lord saw that Leah was unloved, he enabled her
to become pregnant while Rachel remained childless. 32 So
Leah became pregnant and gave birth to a son. She named
him Reuben, for she said, "The Lord has looked with pity
on my oppressed condition. Surely my husband will love me
now." 33 She became pregnant again and had another son.
She said, "Because the Lord heard that I was unloved, he gave
me this one too." So she named him Simeon. 34 She became
pregnant again and had another son. She said, "Now this time
my husband will show me affection, because I have given birth
to three sons for him." That is why he was named Levi. 35
She became pregnant again and had another son. She said,
"This time I will praise the Lord." That is why she named him
Judah. Then she stopped having children. 30:1 When Rachel
saw that she could not give Jacob children, she became jealous
of her sister. She said to Jacob, "Give me children or I'll die!" 2
Jacob became furious with Rachel and exclaimed, "Am I in the
place of God, who has kept you from having children?" 3 She
replied, "Here is my servant Bilhah! Sleep with her so that she
can bear children for me and I can have a family through her."
4 So Rachel gave him her servant Bilhah as a wife, and Jacob
slept with her. 5 Bilhah became pregnant and gave Jacob a son.
6 Then Rachel said, "God has vindicated me. He has responded
to my prayer and given me a son." That is why she named him
Dan. 7 Bilhah, Rachel's servant, became pregnant again and
gave Jacob another son. 8 Then Rachel said, "I have fought
a desperate struggle with my sister, but I have won." So she
named him Naphtali. 9 When Leah saw that she had stopped
having children, she gave her servant Zilpah to Jacob as a wife.
10 Soon Leah's servant Zilpah gave Jacob a son. 11 Leah said,
"How fortunate!" So she named him Gad. 12 Then Leah's
servant Zilpah gave Jacob another son. 13 Leah said, "How

WEEK 2
Monday

Genesis 29:31–30:24 (continued)

happy I am, for women will call me happy!" So she named him
Asher. 14 At the time of the wheat harvest Reuben went out
and found some mandrake plants in a field and brought them
to his mother Leah. Rachel said to Leah, "Give me some of your
son's mandrakes." 15 But Leah replied, "Wasn't it enough that
you've taken away my husband? Would you take away my son's
mandrakes too?" "All right," Rachel said, "he may go to bed with
you tonight in exchange for your son's mandrakes." 16 When
Jacob came in from the fields that evening, Leah went out to
meet him and said, "You must sleep with me because I have paid
for your services with my son's mandrakes." So he went to bed
with her that night. 17 God paid attention to Leah; she became
pregnant and gave Jacob a son for the fifth time. 18 Then Leah
said, "God has granted me a reward because I gave my servant
to my husband as a wife." So she named him Issachar. 19 Leah
became pregnant again and gave Jacob a son for the sixth time.
20 Then Leah said, "God has given me a good gift. Now my
husband will honor me because I have given him six sons."
So she named him Zebulun. 21 After that she gave birth to
a daughter and named her Dinah. 22 Then God took note of
Rachel. He paid attention to her and enabled her to become
pregnant. 23 She became pregnant and gave birth to a son. Then
she said, "God has taken away my shame." 24 She named him
Joseph, saying, "May the LORD give me yet another son."

Colossians 3:1–3

Therefore, if you have been raised with Christ, keep seeking the
things above, where Christ is, seated at the right hand of God.
2 Keep thinking about things above, not things on the earth, 3
for you have died and your life is hidden with Christ in God.

He is always faithful, and He always keeps His promises.

SOAP

WEEK 2 • MONDAY

SOAP / *Colossians 3:1–3*
SCRIPTURE / *Write out the SOAP verses*

OBSERVATION / *Write 3 - 4 observations*

APPLICATION / *Write down 1 - 2 applications*

PRAYER / *Write out a prayer over what you learned*

DEVOTIONAL
WEEK 2 • MONDAY

SOAP

Colossians 3:1–3

Therefore, if you have been raised with Christ, keep seeking the things above, where Christ is, seated at the right hand of God. Keep thinking about things above, not things on earth, for you have died and your life is hidden with Christ in God.

INTO THE TEXT

A consistent theme throughout the latter half of Genesis is the difference between a life that seeks the things of God and one that seeks the things of the world. Jacob and his family members were constantly faced with choices, forcing them to decide whether or not they would choose the things of God. In today's reading, we see how a life that chooses the things of God may include the surrender of our heart's greatest desires.

Leah and Rachel were in constant competition. Rachel was loved by Jacob; Leah was able to have many children. They even used their maid servants to produce more children, as a way of winning against the other. The rivalry between the sisters was a symptom of their weak faith. It showed that their greatest desires were things of the world: the love of a husband and bearing children.

Desiring children or a husband's affection is not in itself sinful. However, when these desires caused Leah and Rachel to compete against one another, use others as objects, and create strife in their family, it led them away from the things of God.

While this rivalry displayed the sisters' weak faith, their confidence in God's character is nevertheless shown by the way they named their children. The children of Israel display the character of God through the names they were given: He remembers and pays attention to the needy, He blesses the oppressed, and He removes the reproach of His people, even if they make a mess along the way.

The narrative of Jacob's family is meant to display how God blessed the family of promise. Jacob's many children show the beginnings of God's promise to make Abraham's descendants as numerous as the stars in the sky. Yet, throughout the narrative, we are distracted by the competition between the sisters. The rivalry distracted the sisters from appreciating the blessing of the many children whom God was giving to Jacob.

Even though Leah and Rachel were often distracted by jealousy and competition, God still poured out His blessings on them. We do nothing to earn any of the gifts He gives us, but He indeed blesses our obedience. The things we desire should not keep us from praising and obeying God; they should drive us closer to Him, either through fervent and desperate cries for help or through glad and thankful worship.

WEEK 2
Tuesday

READ

Genesis 30:25–43

After Rachel had given birth to Joseph, Jacob said to Laban, "Send me on my way so that I can go home to my own country. 26 Let me take my wives and my children whom I have acquired by working for you. Then I'll depart, because you know how hard I've worked for you." 27 But Laban said to him, "If I have found favor in your sight, please stay here, for I have learned by divination that the LORD has blessed me on account of you." 28 He added, "Just name your wages—I'll pay whatever you want." 29 "You know how I have worked for you," Jacob replied, "and how well your livestock have fared under my care. 30 Indeed, you had little before I arrived, but now your possessions have increased many times over. The LORD has blessed you wherever I worked. But now, how long must it be before I do something for my own family too?" 31 So Laban asked, "What should I give you?" "You don't need to give me a thing," Jacob replied, "but if you agree to this one condition, I will continue to care for your flocks and protect them: 32 Let me walk among all your flocks today and remove from them every speckled or spotted sheep, every dark-colored lamb, and the spotted or speckled goats. These animals will be my wages. 33 My integrity will testify for me later on. When you come to verify that I've taken only the wages we agreed on, if I have in my possession any goat that is not speckled or spotted or any sheep that is not dark-colored, it will be considered stolen." 34 "Agreed!" said Laban, "It will be as you say." 35 So that day Laban removed the male goats that were streaked or spotted, all the female goats that were speckled or spotted (all that had any white on them), and all the dark-colored lambs, and put them in the care of his sons. 36 Then he separated them from Jacob by a three-day journey, while Jacob was taking care of the rest of Laban's flocks. 37 But Jacob took fresh-cut branches from poplar, almond, and plane trees. He made white streaks by peeling them, making the white inner wood in the branches visible. 38 Then he set up the peeled

WEEK 2
Tuesday

Genesis 30:25–43 (continued)

branches in all the watering troughs where the flocks came to
drink. He set up the branches in front of the flocks when they
were in heat and came to drink. 39 When the sheep mated in
front of the branches, they gave birth to young that were streaked
or speckled or spotted. 40 Jacob removed these lambs, but he
made the rest of the flock face the streaked and completely dark-
colored animals in Laban's flock. So he made separate flocks for
himself and did not mix them with Laban's flocks. 41 When the
stronger females were in heat, Jacob would set up the branches
in the troughs in front of the flock, so they would mate near the
branches. 42 But if the animals were weaker, he did not set the
branches there. So the weaker animals ended up belonging to
Laban and the stronger animals to Jacob. 43 In this way Jacob
became extremely prosperous. He owned large flocks, male and
female servants, camels, and donkeys.

Proverbs 3:1–12

My child, do not forget my teaching, but let your heart keep my
commandments, 2 for they will provide a long and full life, and
well-being for you. 3 Do not let mercy and truth leave you; bind
them around your neck, write them on the tablet of your heart.
4 Then you will find favor and good understanding, in the sight
of God and people. 5 Trust in the Lord with all your heart, and
do not rely on your own understanding. 6 Acknowledge him in
all your ways, and he will make your paths straight. 7 Do not be
wise in your own estimation; fear the Lord and turn away from
evil. 8 This will bring healing to your body, and refreshment
to your inner self. 9 Honor the Lord from your wealth and
from the firstfruits of all your crops; 10 then your barns will be
filled completely, and your vats will overflow with new wine. 11
My child, do not despise discipline from the Lord, and do not
loathe his rebuke. 12 For the Lord disciplines those he loves,
just as a father disciplines the son in whom he delights.

*When we live
and die based on
God's promises,
death loses
its power.*

SOAP

WEEK 2 • TUESDAY

SOAP / *Proverbs 3:9–10*

SCRIPTURE / *Write out the SOAP verses*

OBSERVATION / *Write 3 - 4 observations*

APPLICATION / *Write down 1 - 2 applications*

PRAYER / *Write out a prayer over what you learned*

SOAP

Proverbs 3:9–10

Honor the Lord from your wealth and from the firstfruits of all your crops; then your barns will be filled completely, and your vats will overflow with new wine.

INTO THE TEXT

Genesis 29 and 30 are a record of Jacob's prosperity; first, his family was enlarged by many children, then his possessions increased, specifically his flocks of sheep and goats. God had promised to bless Jacob and make him great (Genesis 28:13–15) and these events were evidence of God keeping His promise.

In their typical fashion, Jacob and Laban found another opportunity to deceive one another. Both Laban and Jacob recognized the great success that had come to Laban while Jacob worked for him. Now, it was time for Jacob to receive his earnings. In the first act of deception, Laban removed the streaked and spotted sheep and goats from his flocks, making it impossible for Jacob to receive his payment.

Next, Jacob used his own methods to ensure that there were many streaked and spotted sheep and goats in the flocks, especially strong and healthy ones. Whether it was in response to Laban's actions or whether it had been his plan all along, we're not sure. As readers, we wonder if Jacob and Laban's continued deception of one another would ever end! But what is clear is that Jacob prospered even in the midst of Laban's deception.

Jacob recognized the growth of his flocks as God's blessing (Genesis 31:9). Even though he had been deceived and even though he had practiced deceit himself, God blessed Jacob and increased his possessions. It was not Jacob's craftiness that made him prosper, but God's gracious blessing. We will never need to resort to sinful methods to receive God's good gifts. Yet even though Jacob wasn't perfect, God worked on his behalf. God brought justice for Laban's deceit by allowing Jacob to prosper. God overruled both Laban's and Jacob's devices to work out His plan to bless Jacob and his descendants.

Though he relied on his own devices at first, Jacob later recognized his prosperity as God's blessing. When we prosper in our lives, in whatever form, do we recognize it as God's blessing, or as our own success? Self-reliance will harm our faith. When we rely on ourselves for deliverance, blessing, and prosperity, we remove the honor from God that He alone deserves. Choosing the way of God means trusting Him enough to obey Him even when our plans seem like the more reliable option. True blessing can only come from God, and we are called to trust Him for it, no matter what.

WEEK 2
Wednesday

READ

Genesis 31

Jacob heard that Laban's sons were complaining, "Jacob has
taken everything that belonged to our father! He has gotten rich
at our father's expense!" 2 When Jacob saw the look on Laban's
face, he could tell his attitude toward him had changed. 3 The
LORD said to Jacob, "Return to the land of your fathers and to
your relatives. I will be with you." 4 So Jacob sent a message
for Rachel and Leah to come to the field where his flocks were.
5 There he said to them, "I can tell that your father's attitude
toward me has changed, but the God of my father has been with
me. 6 You know that I've worked for your father as hard as I
could, 7 but your father has humiliated me and changed my
wages ten times. But God has not permitted him to do me any
harm. 8 If he said, 'The speckled animals will be your wage,'
then the entire flock gave birth to speckled offspring. But if he
said, 'The streaked animals will be your wage,' then the entire
flock gave birth to streaked offspring. 9 In this way God has
snatched away your father's livestock and given them to me.
10 "Once during breeding season I saw in a dream that the
male goats mating with the flock were streaked, speckled, and
spotted. 11 In the dream the angel of God said to me, 'Jacob!'
'Here I am!' I replied. 12 Then he said, 'Observe that all the
male goats mating with the flock are streaked, speckled, or
spotted, for I have observed all that Laban has done to you. 13
I am the God of Bethel, where you anointed the sacred stone
and made a vow to me. Now leave this land immediately and
return to your native land.'" 14 Then Rachel and Leah replied
to him, "Do we still have any portion or inheritance in our
father's house? 15 Hasn't he treated us like foreigners? He not
only sold us, but completely wasted the money paid for us! 16
Surely all the wealth that God snatched away from our father
belongs to us and to our children. So now do everything God
has told you." 17 So Jacob immediately put his children and his
wives on the camels. 18 He took away all the livestock he had

WEEK 2
Wednesday

Genesis 31 (continued)

acquired in Paddan Aram and all his moveable property that he had accumulated. Then he set out toward the land of Canaan to return to his father Isaac. 19 While Laban had gone to shear his sheep, Rachel stole the household idols that belonged to her father. 20 Jacob also deceived Laban the Aramean by not telling him that he was leaving. 21 He left with all he owned. He quickly crossed the Euphrates River and headed for the hill country of Gilead. 22 Three days later Laban discovered Jacob had left. 23 So he took his relatives with him and pursued Jacob for seven days. He caught up with him in the hill country of Gilead. 24 But God came to Laban the Aramean in a dream at night and warned him, "Be careful that you neither bless nor curse Jacob." 25 Laban overtook Jacob, and when Jacob pitched his tent in the hill country of Gilead, Laban and his relatives set up camp there too. 26 "What have you done?" Laban demanded of Jacob. "You've deceived me and carried away my daughters as if they were captives of war! 27 Why did you run away secretly and deceive me? Why didn't you tell me so I could send you off with a celebration complete with singing, tambourines, and harps? 28 You didn't even allow me to kiss my daughters and my grandchildren goodbye. You have acted foolishly! 29 I have the power to do you harm, but the God of your father told me last night, 'Be careful that you neither bless nor curse Jacob.' 30 Now I understand that you have gone away because you longed desperately for your father's house. Yet why did you steal my gods?" 31 "I left secretly because I was afraid!" Jacob replied to Laban. "I thought you might take your daughters away from me by force. 32 Whoever has taken your gods will be put to death! In the presence of our relatives identify whatever is yours and take it." (Now Jacob did not know that Rachel had stolen them.) 33 So Laban entered Jacob's tent, and Leah's tent, and the tent of the two female servants, but he did not find the idols. Then he left Leah's tent and entered Rachel's. 34 (Now Rachel had taken the idols and put them inside her camel's saddle and sat on them.) Laban searched the whole tent, but did not find

WEEK 2

Wednesday

Genesis 31 (continued)

them. 35 Rachel said to her father, "Don't be angry, my lord. I cannot stand up in your presence because I am having my period." So he searched thoroughly, but did not find the idols. 36 Jacob became angry and argued with Laban. "What did I do wrong?" he demanded of Laban. "What sin of mine prompted you to chase after me in hot pursuit? 37 When you searched through all my goods, did you find anything that belonged to you? Set it here before my relatives and yours,and let them settle the dispute between the two of us! 38 "I have been with you for the past twenty years. Your ewes and female goats have not miscarried, nor have I eaten rams from your flocks. 39 Animals torn by wild beasts I never brought to you; I always absorbed the loss myself. You always made me pay for every missing animal, whether it was taken by day or at night. 40 I was consumed by scorching heat during the day and by piercing cold at night, and I went without sleep. 41 This was my lot for twenty years in your house: I worked like a slave for you—fourteen years for your two daughters and six years for your flocks—but you changed my wages ten times! 42 If the God of my father—the God of Abraham, the one whom Isaac fears—had not been with me, you would certainly have sent me away empty-handed! But God saw how I was oppressed and how hard I worked, and he rebuked you last night." 43 Laban replied to Jacob, "These women are my daughters, these children are my grandchildren, and these flocks are my flocks. All that you see belongs to me. But how can I harm these daughters of mine today or the children to whom they have given birth? 44 So now, come, let's make a formal agreement, you and I, and it will be proof that we have made peace." 45 So Jacob took a stone and set it up as a memorial pillar. 46 Then he said to his relatives, "Gather stones." So they brought stones and put them in a pile. They ate there by the pile of stones. 47 Laban called it Jegar Sahadutha, but Jacob called it Galeed. 48 Laban said, "This pile of stones is a witness of our agreement today." That is why it was called Galeed. 49 It was also called Mizpah because he said, "May the LORD watch between

WEEK 2
Wednesday

Genesis 31 (continued)

us when we are out of sight of one another. 50 If you mistreat my daughters or if you take wives besides my daughters, although no one else is with us, realize that God is witness to your actions." 51 "Here is this pile of stones and this pillar I have set up between me and you," Laban said to Jacob. 52 "This pile of stones and the pillar are reminders that I will not pass beyond this pile to come to harm you and that you will not pass beyond this pile and this pillar to come to harm me. 53 May the God of Abraham and the god of Nahor, the gods of their father, judge between us." Jacob took an oath by the God whom his father Isaac feared. 54 Then Jacob offered a sacrifice on the mountain and invited his relatives to eat the meal. They ate the meal and spent the night on the mountain. 55 (32:1) Early in the morning Laban kissed his grandchildren and his daughters goodbye and blessed them. Then Laban left and returned home.

1 John 3:18–24

Little children, let us not love with word or with tongue but in deed and truth. 19 And by this we will know that we are of the truth and will convince our conscience in his presence, 20 that if our conscience condemns us, that God is greater than our conscience and knows all things. 21 Dear friends, if our conscience does not condemn us, we have confidence in the presence of God, 22 and whatever we ask we receive from him, because we keep his commandments and do the things that are pleasing to him. 23 Now this is his commandment: that we believe in the name of his Son Jesus Christ and love one another, just as he gave us the commandment. 24 And the person who keeps his commandments resides in God, and God in him. Now by this we know that God resides in us: by the Spirit he has given us.

He is the one who makes the promise, and He is the one who is faithful to keep it.

SOAP

WEEK 2 • WEDNESDAY

SOAP / *1 John 3:23–24*
SCRIPTURE / *Write out the SOAP verses*

OBSERVATION / *Write 3 - 4 observations*

APPLICATION / *Write down 1 - 2 applications*

PRAYER / *Write out a prayer over what you learned*

DEVOTIONAL

WEEK 2 • WEDNESDAY

SOAP

1 John 3:23–24

Now this is his commandment: that we believe in the name of his Son Jesus Christ and love one another, just as he gave us the commandment. And the person who keeps his commandments resides in God, and God in him. Now by this we know that God resides in us: by the Spirit he has given us.

INTO THE TEXT

When we study Genesis from a literary perspective, we learn a lot about Jacob. Jacob is the protagonist, the person who changes in the narrative. Laban is the antagonist, the person who causes the change in the protagonist.

A great change did take place in Jacob through his time in Paddan Aram. Jacob arrived as a deceiver who had been given a great promise from God. Through God's discipline and through experiencing deceit himself by Laban, Jacob's identity as a deceiver seemed to have changed. Jacob recognized how God had blessed Him: by His grace alone.

God met Jacob in a dream at Bethel, promising to bless and protect him, and Jacob responded by promising to return to the land of his father (Genesis 28:10–22). At this point, God met Jacob in a second dream and instructed him to take his family and his possessions and return to the land. Jacob obeyed.

When Jacob recognized the way God kept His promise, he was faithful to fulfill the vow he made to God. Though Jacob was not perfect, these events show how he was turning to God and away from his own devices. Instead of continuing to battle with Laban, Jacob left, obeying God's instruction. God commanded Jacob's return, so God's protection of him and his family was certain. God's blessings had been poured out on Jacob through dreams, discipline, a family, and many possessions, and it was time for Jacob to change, to act in obedience, and to follow God.

No matter our past, no matter how many times we've acted like Jacob, deceiving others or trusting in our own devices, we can always choose to be obedient to God. Whether it is the first time we have turned to Him or whether we are returning to Him, He is always willing to forgive us. We can turn to Him and commit to faithfulness, certain He will be gracious.

Jacob was obedient to God's specific command to return home. We have been clearly commanded by God to believe in His Son Jesus Christ and to love one another. When we follow God's commands, we can be certain of His protection. For when He chooses to bless us and we are obedient to Him by believing in His Son, we can be confident that His love and grace will cover our lives.

WEEK 2
Thursday

READ

Genesis 32:1–21

So Jacob went on his way and the angels of God met him.
2 When Jacob saw them, he exclaimed, "This is the camp
of God!" So he named that place Mahanaim. 3 Jacob sent
messengers on ahead to his brother Esau in the land of Seir,
the region of Edom. 4 He commanded them, "This is what
you must say to my lord Esau: 'This is what your servant
Jacob says: I have been staying with Laban until now. 5 I
have oxen, donkeys, sheep, and male and female servants. I
have sent this message to inform my lord, so that I may find
favor in your sight.'" 6 The messengers returned to Jacob
and said, "We went to your brother Esau. He is coming
to meet you and has 400 men with him." 7 Jacob was
very afraid and upset. So he divided the people who were
with him into two camps, as well as the flocks, herds, and
camels. 8 "If Esau attacks one camp," he thought, "then the
other camp will be able to escape." 9 Then Jacob prayed,
"O God of my father Abraham, God of my father Isaac, O
LORD, you said to me, 'Return to your land and to your
relatives and I will make you prosper.' 10 I am not worthy
of all the faithful love you have shown your servant. With
only my walking stick I crossed the Jordan, but now I have
become two camps. 11 Rescue me, I pray, from the hand of
my brother Esau, for I am afraid he will come and attack
me, as well as the mothers with their children. 12 But you
said, 'I will certainly make you prosper and will make your
descendants like the sand on the seashore, too numerous to
count.'" 13 Jacob stayed there that night. Then he sent as
a gift to his brother Esau 14 200 female goats and 20 male
goats, 200 ewes and 20 rams, 15 30 female camels with
their young, 40 cows and 10 bulls, and 20 female donkeys
and 10 male donkeys. 16 He entrusted them to his servants,

WEEK 2
Thursday

Genesis 32:1–21 (continued)

who divided them into herds. He told his servants, "Pass over before me, and keep some distance between one herd and the next." 17 He instructed the servant leading the first herd, "When my brother Esau meets you and asks, 'To whom do you belong? Where are you going? Whose herds are you driving?' 18 then you must say, 'They belong to your servant Jacob. They have been sent as a gift to my lord Esau. In fact Jacob himself is behind us.'" 19 He also gave these instructions to the second and third servants, as well as all those who were following the herds, saying, "You must say the same thing to Esau when you meet him. 20 You must also say, 'In fact your servant Jacob is behind us.'" Jacob thought, "I will first appease him by sending a gift ahead of me. After that I will meet him. Perhaps he will accept me." 21 So the gifts were sent on ahead of him while he spent that night in the camp.

Psalm 56:3–4

When I am afraid, I trust in you. 4 In God—I boast in his promise— in God I trust; I am not afraid. What can mere men do to me?

Psalm 56:10–11

In God—I boast in his promise— in the Lord—I boast in his promise— 11 in God I trust; I am not afraid. What can mere men do to me?

He redeems, restores, and rebuilds even the most shattered of hearts, relationships, communities, and nations.

SOAP

WEEK 2 • THURSDAY

SOAP / *Psalm 56:3–4*
SCRIPTURE / *Write out the SOAP verses*

OBSERVATION / *Write 3 - 4 observations*

APPLICATION / *Write down 1 - 2 applications*

PRAYER / *Write out a prayer over what you learned*

SOAP

Psalm 56:3–4

When I am afraid, I trust in you. In God—I boast in his promise—in God I trust; I am not afraid. What can mere men do to me?

INTO THE TEXT

God was with Jacob. God called him out of a foreign land to return to the land of promise, the land of his fathers. God protected Jacob from harm, keeping Laban, his father-in-law and enemy, from harming him or his family. Jacob was walking in obedience, fulfilling his vow to return to the promised land and walk with his God.

But then Esau, his brother and first enemy, was closing in. Even though God protected him from Laban, Jacob was very afraid and upset. He had stolen the blessing of the firstborn from his brother, and the last time they saw one another, Esau had vowed to kill him.

Very early in Jacob's life, his shrewd character was revealed. He was cunning and clever, skilled at getting what he wanted. He knew how to manipulate a situation or deceive a person to accomplish his plans. Until this point, there is no record of him seeking God's help. The scenes surrounding this event show the development of Jacob's character. He trusted God to protect him from Laban, and he was obedient to God's command to return to the land. In all of the previous situations that Jacob manipulated, it is never recorded that he prayed before acting. Yet, now, when his first enemy was coming his way with 400 men, Jacob sought God's protection and deliverance.

Even though he was beginning to change, Jacob still developed a plan to save himself. The gifts he set aside for Esau were an attempt to repay him for the blessing he had stolen years earlier. Jacob sought to appease his brother by giving him a large portion of the blessing that God had appointed to him, not Esau. Jacob's gift shows he was so afraid of Esau's wrath that he was willing to give up what God had divinely given him. Jacob asked God for rescue but then tried to rescue himself.

How often do we, like Jacob, seek God's protection, provision, or wisdom and then continue with our plans? As we seek to choose the things of God and not the things of the world, we must recognize that we often have to wait for God's answer. His plans are never thwarted, His blessings never delayed, but our tendency to be afraid and upset can easily cause us to rely on ourselves for deliverance. Instead of trusting His timing, we might take extreme measures to guarantee our rescue. May we trust God in all circumstances and wait for His deliverance.

WEEK 2
Friday

READ

Genesis 32:22–32

During the night Jacob quickly took his two wives, his
two female servants, and his eleven sons and crossed the
ford of the Jabbok. 23 He took them and sent them across
the stream along with all his possessions. 24 So Jacob was
left alone. Then a man wrestled with him until daybreak.
25 When the man saw that he could not defeat Jacob, he
struck the socket of his hip so the socket of Jacob's hip was
dislocated while he wrestled with him. 26 Then the man
said, "Let me go, for the dawn is breaking." "I will not let
you go," Jacob replied, "unless you bless me." 27 The man
asked him, "What is your name?" He answered, "Jacob." 28
"No longer will your name be Jacob," the man told him,
"but Israel, because you have fought with God and with
men and have prevailed." 29 Then Jacob asked, "Please
tell me your name." "Why do you ask my name?" the man
replied. Then he blessed Jacob there. 30 So Jacob named
the place Peniel, explaining, "Certainly I have seen God
face to face and have survived." 31 The sun rose over him
as he crossed over Penuel, but he was limping because of his
hip. 32 That is why to this day the Israelites do not eat the
sinew which is attached to the socket of the hip, because
he struck the socket of Jacob's hip near the attached sinew.

SOAP

WEEK 2 • FRIDAY

SOAP / *Genesis 32:28*

SCRIPTURE / *Write out the SOAP verses*

OBSERVATION / *Write 3 - 4 observations*

APPLICATION / *Write down 1 - 2 applications*

PRAYER / *Write out a prayer over what you learned*

SOAP

Genesis 32:28

"No longer will your name be Jacob," the man told him, "but Israel, because you have fought with God and with men and have prevailed."

INTO THE TEXT

In Hebrew, Jacob's name is pronounced *Ya'aqob*. It sounds like the word *'aqab*, which means "to grasp the heel" or "to deceive." *'Aqab* literally means "to grasp the heel" but it was used figuratively to describe deception or metaphorically to suggest tripping someone up by their heels. Jacob literally seized his twin brother's heel at his birth, and he figuratively seized heels for much of his life.

Jacob was a deceiver. He deceived his brother, Esau, his father, Isaac, and his uncle and father-in-law, Laban. Being a deceiver had become Jacob's identity. It was even his name. Yet, in the last few scenes that we've read, the author of Genesis described a change taking place in Jacob. He obeyed God and returned to the land of his fathers. Then, he prayed and asked God for deliverance from his brother Esau. His behavior was changing. But the night at the Jabbok river was the night that would ultimately change Jacob's identity.

Jacob wrestled with a man that night. Before the sun rose, the man told Jacob to let him go. When Jacob refused to let him go without a blessing, the man asked his name. Jacob again faced the reality of who he was: a deceiver. At that moment, God changed his identity: "No longer will your name be Jacob . . . but Israel, because you have fought with God and with men and have prevailed."

At that moment, God gave Jacob a new identity. God marked Jacob for who he would become, not who he had been. God gave him a new identity as a promise of what He would continue to do. God would continue to fulfill his promise to Jacob, blessing him as He did his father and grandfather. Jacob would receive the blessing, and God would still get the glory. Jacob was crippled the night before he would face his first enemy; he faced the man who had vowed to kill him, and he was physically impaired. Jacob could not be delivered by his own strength. God made it clear to Jacob that He alone was his source of deliverance; He alone would do it.

It is incredibly gracious of God to rid us of our self-reliance. God will accomplish His purposes by His power alone. He does not need our help to fulfill His plans or keep His promises. No matter the plans we might create, God will make it clear that it is He alone who delivers us, He alone who saves.

REFLECT

WEEK 2

1. *What are some of the great blessings God has given you? List as many as you can. Are you more prone to celebrate these blessings or compare the blessings you have received with the blessings others have received from God? How can you fight a spirit of comparison today?*

2. *Do you acknowledge God as the source of all your success? In what area of your life do you tend to rely on your own devices instead of trusting God's plan?*

3. *Are you obedient to God's commands? Have you believed in His Son? Do you love others? Do you love others even when they are unkind to you or attempt to deceive or overpower you?*

4. *In what area of your life do you often ask God for deliverance but then create your own rescue plans? What would happen if you waited on God for deliverance?*

5. *In what ways has God transformed your identity? In what ways have you seen God strip you of self-reliance?*

JOURNAL

your thoughts

JOURNAL

your thoughts

"Look! I have set
before you today
life and prosperity
on the one hand, and
death and disaster
on the other. What
I am commanding you
today is to love the
LORD your God, to
walk in his ways, and to
obey his commandments,
his statutes, and his
ordinances. Then you
will live and become
numerous and the LORD
your God will bless you
in the land that you
are about to possess."

Deuteronomy 30:15-16

PRAY

Write down your prayer requests and praises for this week.

WEEKLY CHALLENGE

Reflect on the events in Jacob's life you have read so far. Would God have delivered Jacob without Jacob's shrewd behavior? Did Jacob miss out on the blessing of God through self-reliance and deception? How did Jacob's children display the same tendencies of self-reliance and deception?

WEEK 3
Monday

READ

Genesis 33

Jacob looked up and saw that Esau was coming along with 400 men. So he divided the children among Leah, Rachel, and the two female servants. 2 He put the servants and their children in front, with Leah and her children behind them, and Rachel and Joseph behind them. 3 But Jacob himself went on ahead of them, and he bowed toward the ground seven times as he approached his brother. 4 But Esau ran to meet him, embraced him, hugged his neck, and kissed him. Then they both wept. 5 When Esau looked up and saw the women and the children, he asked, "Who are these people with you?" Jacob replied, "The children whom God has graciously given your servant." 6 The female servants came forward with their children and bowed down. 7 Then Leah came forward with her children and they bowed down. Finally Joseph and Rachel came forward and bowed down. 8 Esau then asked, "What did you intend by sending all these herds to meet me?" Jacob replied, "To find favor in your sight, my lord." 9 But Esau said, "I have plenty, my brother. Keep what belongs to you." 10 "No, please take them," Jacob said. "If I have found favor in your sight, accept my gift from my hand. Now that I have seen your face and you have accepted me, it is as if I have seen the face of God. 11 Please take my present that was brought to you, for God has been generous to me and I have all I need." When Jacob urged him, he took it. 12 Then Esau said, "Let's be on our way! I will go in front of you." 13 But Jacob said to him, "My lord knows that the children are young, and that I have to look after the sheep and cattle that are nursing their young. If they are driven too hard for even a single day, all the animals will die. 14 Let my lord go on ahead of his servant. I will travel more slowly,

WEEK 3
Monday

Genesis 33 (continued)

at the pace of the herds and the children, until I come to my lord at Seir." 15 So Esau said, "Let me leave some of my men with you." "Why do that?" Jacob replied. "My lord has already been kind enough to me." 16 So that same day Esau made his way back to Seir. 17 But Jacob traveled to Sukkoth where he built himself a house and made shelters for his livestock. That is why the place was called Sukkoth. 18 After he left Paddan Aram, Jacob came safely to the city of Shechem in the land of Canaan, and he camped near the city. 19 Then he purchased the portion of the field where he had pitched his tent; he bought it from the sons of Hamor, Shechem's father, for 100 pieces of money. 20 There he set up an altar and called it "The God of Israel is God."

2 Corinthians 5:16–21

So then from now on we acknowledge no one from an outward human point of view. Even though we have known Christ from such a human point of view, now we do not know him in that way any longer. 17 So then, if anyone is in Christ, he is a new creation; what is old has passed away—look, what is new has come! 18 And all these things are from God who reconciled us to himself through Christ, and who has given us the ministry of reconciliation. 19 In other words, in Christ God was reconciling the world to himself, not counting people's trespasses against them, and he has given us the message of reconciliation. 20 Therefore we are ambassadors for Christ, as though God were making his plea through us. We plead with you on Christ's behalf, "Be reconciled to God!" 21 God made the one who did not know sin to be sin for us, so that in him we would become the righteousness of God.

A life that chooses the things of God may include the surrender of our heart's greatest desires.

SOAP

WEEK 3 • MONDAY

SOAP / *2 Corinthians 5:18–19*
SCRIPTURE / *Write out the SOAP verses*

OBSERVATION / *Write 3 - 4 observations*

APPLICATION / *Write down 1 - 2 applications*

PRAYER / *Write out a prayer over what you learned*

SOAP

2 Corinthians 5:18–19

And all these things are from God who reconciled us to himself through Christ, and who has given us the ministry of reconciliation. In other words, in Christ God was reconciling the world to himself, not counting people's trespasses against them, and he has given us the message of reconciliation.

INTO THE TEXT

When Jacob began his journey back to the land of his fathers, he seemed to be moving away from his life of deception and trickery. He was reconciled to God during the night at Peniel when he was blessed and given a new name. Jacob did nothing to deserve this grace.

Jacob and Esau reunited, but they each perceived their reconciliation in a vastly different way. Esau greeted Jacob as a brother. Esau recognized how he, too, had been blessed, and he did not need Jacob's gift. He offered to protect Jacob, his family, and his possessions, showing kindness and love to his brother. In contrast, Jacob greeted Esau as a servant. Jacob submitted himself to Esau, offering gifts as restitution for his past wrongs. God displayed His continued protection of Jacob through his reconciliation with Esau.

God's work was evident throughout Jacob's journey home. The reconciliation between Jacob and Esau was an incredible act of grace. God changed Esau's heart and attitude toward the brother who had wronged him. And God worked in both brothers to bring about this reconciliation. Esau turned from seeking revenge to embracing his brother, and Jacob turned from pride and a feeling of entitlement to humility and generosity. This reconciliation was a gift of God and He alone brought it about.

We, too, need reconciliation. Because of sin, we need to be reconciled to God, yet there is nothing we can do to bring this about. It is God, by His incredible grace, who reconciles us to Himself. We are reconciled to God when we place our faith in His Son. And because of His gift of reconciliation, we too can be reconciled to others. Choosing to be at peace with others is one of the ways we choose the things of God. For He has given us a great message to the world of forgiveness and reconciliation. It is not a normal, human response to conflict, yet, through the ministry of Christ, we can be reconciled to others, relying on God alone to do the work of redeeming even the most broken relationships.

WEEK 3
Tuesday

READ

Genesis 34

Now Dinah, Leah's daughter whom she bore to Jacob, went
to meet the young women of the land. 2 When Shechem
son of Hamor the Hivite, who ruled that area, saw her, he
grabbed her, forced himself on her, and sexually assaulted
her. 3 Then he became very attached to Dinah, Jacob's
daughter. He fell in love with the young woman and spoke
romantically to her. 4 Shechem said to his father Hamor,
"Acquire this young girl as my wife." 5 When Jacob heard
that Shechem had violated his daughter Dinah, his sons
were with the livestock in the field. So Jacob remained silent
until they came in. 6 Then Shechem's father Hamor went
to speak with Jacob about Dinah. 7 Now Jacob's sons had
come in from the field when they heard the news. They were
offended and very angry because Shechem had disgraced
Israel by sexually assaulting Jacob's daughter, a crime that
should not be committed. 8 But Hamor made this appeal
to them: "My son Shechem is in love with your daughter.
Please give her to him as his wife. 9 Intermarry with us.
Let us marry your daughters, and take our daughters as
wives for yourselves. 10 You may live among us, and the
land will be open to you. Live in it, travel freely in it, and
acquire property in it." 11 Then Shechem said to Dinah's
father and brothers, "Let me find favor in your sight, and
whatever you require of me I'll give. 12 You can make the
bride price and the gift I must bring very expensive, and
I'll give whatever you ask of me. Just give me the young
woman as my wife!" 13 Jacob's sons answered Shechem
and his father Hamor deceitfully when they spoke because
Shechem had violated their sister Dinah. 14 They said

WEEK 3

Tuesday

Genesis 34 (continued)

to them, "We cannot give our sister to a man who is not circumcised, for it would be a disgrace to us. 15 We will give you our consent on this one condition: You must become like us by circumcising all your males. 16 Then we will give you our daughters to marry, and we will take your daughters as wives for ourselves, and we will live among you and become one people. 17 But if you do not agree to our terms by being circumcised, then we will take our sister and depart." 18 Their offer pleased Hamor and his son Shechem. 19 The young man did not delay in doing what they asked because he wanted Jacob's daughter Dinah badly. (Now he was more important than anyone in his father's household.) 20 So Hamor and his son Shechem went to the gate of their city and spoke to the men of their city, 21 "These men are at peace with us. So let them live in the land and travel freely in it, for the land is wide enough for them. We will take their daughters for wives, and we will give them our daughters to marry. 22 Only on this one condition will these men consent to live with us and become one people: They demand that every male among us be circumcised just as they are circumcised. 23 If we do so, won't their livestock, their property, and all their animals become ours? So let's consent to their demand, so they will live among us." 24 All the men who assembled at the city gate agreed with Hamor and his son Shechem. Every male who assembled at the city gate was circumcised. 25 In three days, when they were still in pain, two of Jacob's sons, Simeon and Levi, Dinah's brothers, each took his sword and went to the unsuspecting city and slaughtered every male. 26 They killed Hamor and his son Shechem

Genesis 34 (continued)

with the sword, took Dinah from Shechem's house, and left. 27 Jacob's sons killed them and looted the city because their sister had been violated. 28 They took their flocks, herds, and donkeys, as well as everything in the city and in the surrounding fields. 29 They captured as plunder all their wealth, all their little ones, and their wives, including everything in the houses. 30 Then Jacob said to Simeon and Levi, "You have brought ruin on me by making me a foul odor among the inhabitants of the land—among the Canaanites and the Perizzites. I am few in number; they will join forces against me and attack me, and both I and my family will be destroyed!" 31 But Simeon and Levi replied, "Should he treat our sister like a common prostitute?"

Romans 12:17–21

Do not repay anyone evil for evil; consider what is good before all people. 18 If possible, so far as it depends on you, live peaceably with all people. 19 Do not avenge yourselves, dear friends, but give place to God's wrath, for it is written, "***Vengeance is mine, I will repay***," says the Lord. 20 Rather, ***if your enemy is hungry, feed him; if he is thirsty, give him a drink; for in doing this you will be heaping burning coals on his head***. 21 Do not be overcome by evil, but overcome evil with good.

SOAP

WEEK 3 • TUESDAY

SOAP / *Romans 12:19*

SCRIPTURE / *Write out the SOAP verses*

OBSERVATION / *Write 3 - 4 observations*

APPLICATION / *Write down 1 - 2 applications*

PRAYER / *Write out a prayer over what you learned*

DEVOTIONAL

WEEK 3 • TUESDAY

SOAP

Romans 12:19

Do not avenge yourselves, dear friends, but give place to God's wrath, for it is written, "Vengeance is mine, I will repay," says the Lord.

INTO THE TEXT

The events recorded in Genesis 34 are horrific and evil. The violent rape of Dinah shows the evil and lawlessness of the Canaanite people, a people whom God would destroy through the descendants of Israel. The lack of response to the news of the crimes against his only daughter shows indecisiveness and passiveness in Jacob at best, at worst, a lack of love and care for the children of Leah.

When Jacob did not deal with Dina's attacker as justice demanded, her brothers Simeon and Levi stepped in. While the resulting violence was not right, it was a response to both the horrible crime of Shechem and the passivity of their father. Simeon and Levi understood that Dinah's defilement could not be ignored. Their response showed deep care and concern for both her safety and reputation, as well as great love for her.

Simeon and Levi deceived Shechem and Hamor, a tactic no doubt learned from their father. They plotted vengeance against Shechem, but there is no record of them seeking God's direction or help, another behavior modeled many times by Jacob. While their desire for justice was good, their methods of vengeance were not the ways of God.

The evil done to Dinah was inexcusable. Jacob's inactivity led to acts of vengeance from her brothers. While their desire for justice was godly, their methods of vengeance were worldly. Had the brothers responded in faith, they would have sought God for guidance about how to deal justly with Shechem, for He is a God of justice (see Deuteronomy 22:25–28). He promises to repay the wicked for their crimes, giving full vent to His wrath when we trust His vengeance.

This is not an easy account to study, and it may leave us angry or confused. God promised to protect and deliver Jacob's family—that included justice for Dinah. When we face injustice, we can be confident that God will work on our behalf. He promises that He will repay the wicked for what they have done. His justice is never misplaced, never misapplied. He is always fighting for His children. Unfortunately, we did not get to see God deal with sin according to His perfect wisdom in these events because Dinah's brothers relied on their furious vengeance. May we, on the other hand, have enough faith to wait for God's perfect timing and method of working justice on our behalf.

WEEK 3
Wednesday

READ

Genesis 35

Then God said to Jacob, "Go up at once to Bethel and live there. Make an altar there to God, who appeared to you when you fled from your brother Esau." 2 So Jacob told his household and all who were with him, "Get rid of the foreign gods you have among you. Purify yourselves and change your clothes. 3 Let us go up at once to Bethel. Then I will make an altar there to God, who responded to me in my time of distress and has been with me wherever I went." 4 So they gave Jacob all the foreign gods that were in their possession and the rings that were in their ears. Jacob buried them under the oak near Shechem 5 and they started on their journey. The surrounding cities were afraid of God, and they did not pursue the sons of Jacob. 6 Jacob and all those who were with him arrived at Luz (that is, Bethel) in the land of Canaan. 7 He built an altar there and named the place El Bethel because there God had revealed himself to him when he was fleeing from his brother. 8 (Deborah, Rebekah's nurse, died and was buried under the oak below Bethel; thus it was named Oak of Weeping.) 9 God appeared to Jacob again after he returned from Paddan Aram and blessed him. 10 God said to him, "Your name is Jacob, but your name will no longer be called Jacob; Israel will be your name." So God named him Israel. 11 Then God said to him, "I am the Sovereign God. Be fruitful and multiply! A nation—even a company of nations—will descend from you; kings will be among your descendants! 12 The land I gave to Abraham and Isaac I will give to you. To your descendants I will also give this land." 13 Then God went up from the place where he spoke with him. 14 So Jacob set up a sacred stone pillar in the place where God spoke with him. He poured out a drink offering on it, and then he poured oil on it. 15 Jacob named the place where God spoke with him Bethel. 16 They traveled on from Bethel, and when Ephrath was still some distance away, Rachel went into labor—and her labor was hard. 17 When her labor was at its hardest, the midwife said to her, "Don't be afraid, for you are having another son." 18 With her dying breath, she named him Ben

WEEK 3
Wednesday

Genesis 35 (continued)

Oni. But his father called him Benjamin instead. 19 So Rachel died
and was buried on the way to Ephrath (that is, Bethlehem). 20 Jacob
set up a marker over her grave; it is the Marker of Rachel's Grave
to this day. 21 Then Israel traveled on and pitched his tent beyond
Migdal Eder. 22 While Israel was living in that land, Reuben went
to bed with Bilhah, his father's concubine, and Israel heard about
it. Jacob had twelve sons: 23 The sons of Leah were Reuben, Jacob's
firstborn, as well as Simeon, Levi, Judah, Issachar, and Zebulun. 24
The sons of Rachel were Joseph and Benjamin. 25 The sons of Bilhah,
Rachel's servant, were Dan and Naphtali. 26 The sons of Zilpah,
Leah's servant, were Gad and Asher. These were the sons of Jacob
who were born to him in Paddan Aram. 27 So Jacob came back to
his father Isaac in Mamre, to Kiriath Arba (that is, Hebron), where
Abraham and Isaac had stayed. 28 Isaac lived to be 180 years old. 29
Then Isaac breathed his last and joined his ancestors. He died an old
man who had lived a full life. His sons Esau and Jacob buried him.

Deuteronomy 30:15–20

"Look! I have set before you today life and prosperity on the
one hand, and death and disaster on the other. 16 What I am
commanding you today is to love the LORD your God, to walk in
his ways, and to obey his commandments, his statutes, and his
ordinances. Then you will live and become numerous and the LORD
your God will bless you in the land that you are about to possess. 17
However, if you turn aside and do not obey, but are lured away to
worship and serve other gods, 18 I declare to you this very day that
you will certainly perish! You will not extend your time in the land
you are crossing the Jordan to possess. 19 Today I invoke heaven and
earth as witnesses against you that I have set life and death, blessing
and curse, before you. Therefore choose life so that you and your
descendants may live! 20 I also call on you to love the LORD your
God, to obey him and be loyal to him, for he gives you life and
enables you to live continually in the land the LORD promised to
give to your ancestors Abraham, Isaac, and Jacob."

True blessing can only come from God, and we are called to trust Him for it, no matter what.

SOAP

WEEK 3 • WEDNESDAY

SOAP / *Deuteronomy 30:15–16*

SCRIPTURE / *Write out the SOAP verses*

OBSERVATION / *Write 3 - 4 observations*

APPLICATION / *Write down 1 - 2 applications*

PRAYER / *Write out a prayer over what you learned*

SOAP

Deuteronomy 30:15–16

"Look! I have set before you today life and prosperity on the one hand, and death and disaster on the other. What I am commanding you today is to love the LORD your God, to walk in his ways, and to obey his commandments, his statutes, and his ordinances. Then you will live and become numerous and the LORD your God will bless you in the land that you are about to possess."

INTO THE TEXT

Genesis 35 serves as the conclusion in the narrative of Jacob. While Jacob is mentioned many more times throughout the remainder of Genesis, the focus of the narrative now turns to his children. The author of Genesis closed the lives of Abraham and Isaac in similar ways, not with their deaths, but with a transition to their sons as the subject and as heir to the promise.

Jacob's life was full of success and failure, of blessing, discipline, conflict, resolution, and grace. Jacob was not a perfect man, husband, father, friend, brother, or son. In spite of all his failures and shortcomings, he was still chosen by God. By grace, God chose to bless Jacob over Esau. By grace, God promised to be with Jacob as He had been with his father and grandfather. By grace, God gave Jacob twelve sons and one daughter. By grace, God increased Jacob's possessions. By grace, God brought Jacob back to the land of promise. By grace, God reconciled Jacob to his brother. And by grace, God would continue to bless and be with Jacob's descendants.

As we reflect on Jacob's life, we find one central theme: choosing the things of God over the things of the world. God continually gave Jacob opportunities to choose the things of God and reject the desires of the flesh and the ways of the world. Sometimes, Jacob did choose the things of God. Other times, he turned to his own devices and worldly ways for his deliverance. But like Jacob, we are continually faced with these choices; it is a daily decision. Today, we can set aside idols, false gods, desires of the flesh, and self-reliance and instead choose to follow God, finding blessing, protection, and fulfilled promises in Him.

Many years later, when Jacob's family had become a nation, they had to deal with this same decision. As they entered the land of Canaan to take it as their own, fulfilling the promise God had made generations before, they faced this choice: life and prosperity by obedience to God or death and destruction by going their own way. Every day we have the opportunity to choose the things of God over the things of the world. And no matter how many times we have chosen disobedience, we can still turn back to the God of promise and choose life in Him.

WEEK 3
Thursday

READ

Genesis 36:1—37:1

What follows is the account of Esau (also known as Edom). 2
Esau took his wives from the Canaanites: Adah the daughter of
Elon the Hittite, and Oholibamah the daughter of Anah and
granddaughter of Zibeon the Hivite, 3 in addition to Basemath
the daughter of Ishmael and sister of Nebaioth. 4 Adah bore
Eliphaz to Esau, Basemath bore Reuel, 5 and Oholibamah bore
Jeush, Jalam, and Korah. These were the sons of Esau who were
born to him in the land of Canaan. 6 Esau took his wives, his
sons, his daughters, all the people in his household, his livestock,
his animals, and all his possessions that he had acquired in the
land of Canaan, and he went to a land some distance away from
Jacob his brother 7 because they had too many possessions to be
able to stay together, and the land where they had settled was not
able to support them because of their livestock. 8 So Esau (also
known as Edom) lived in the hill country of Seir. 9 This is the
account of Esau, the father of the Edomites, in the hill country
of Seir. 10 These were the names of Esau's sons: Eliphaz, the son
of Esau's wife Adah, and Reuel, the son of Esau's wife Basemath.
11 These were the sons of Eliphaz: Teman, Omar, Zepho, Gatam,
and Kenaz. 12 Timna, a concubine of Esau's son Eliphaz, bore
Amalek to Eliphaz. These were the sons of Esau's wife Adah. 13
These were the sons of Reuel: Nahath, Zerah, Shammah, and
Mizzah. These were the sons of Esau's wife Basemath. 14 These
were the sons of Esau's wife Oholibamah the daughter of Anah
and granddaughter of Zibeon: She bore Jeush, Jalam, and Korah
to Esau. 15 These were the chiefs among the descendants of
Esau, the sons of Eliphaz, Esau's firstborn: chief Teman, chief
Omar, chief Zepho, chief Kenaz, 16 chief Korah, chief Gatam,
chief Amalek. These were the chiefs descended from Eliphaz in
the land of Edom; these were the sons of Adah. 17 These were
the sons of Esau's son Reuel: chief Nahath, chief Zerah, chief
Shammah, chief Mizzah. These were the chiefs descended from

WEEK 3
Thursday

Genesis 36:1—37:1 (continued)

Reuel in the land of Edom; these were the sons of Esau's wife
Basemath. 18 These were the sons of Esau's wife Oholibamah:
chief Jeush, chief Jalam, chief Korah. These were the chiefs
descended from Esau's wife Oholibamah, the daughter of Anah.
19 These were the sons of Esau (also known as Edom), and these
were their chiefs. 20 These were the sons of Seir the Horite,
who were living in the land: Lotan, Shobal, Zibeon, Anah, 21
Dishon, Ezer, and Dishan. These were the chiefs of the Horites,
the descendants of Seir in the land of Edom. 22 The sons of
Lotan were Hori and Homam; Lotan's sister was Timna. 23
These were the sons of Shobal: Alvan, Manahath, Ebal, Shepho,
and Onam. 24 These were the sons of Zibeon: Aiah and Anah
(who discovered the hot springs in the wilderness as he pastured
the donkeys of his father Zibeon). 25 These were the children
of Anah: Dishon and Oholibamah, the daughter of Anah. 26
These were the sons of Dishon: Hemdan, Eshban, Ithran, and
Keran. 27 These were the sons of Ezer: Bilhan, Zaavan, and
Akan. 28 These were the sons of Dishan: Uz and Aran. 29 These
were the chiefs of the Horites: chief Lotan, chief Shobal, chief
Zibeon, chief Anah, 30 chief Dishon, chief Ezer, chief Dishan.
These were the chiefs of the Horites, according to their chief
lists in the land of Seir. 31 These were the kings who reigned
in the land of Edom before any king ruled over the Israelites:
32 Bela the son of Beor reigned in Edom; the name of his city
was Dinhabah. 33 When Bela died, Jobab the son of Zerah from
Bozrah reigned in his place. 34 When Jobab died, Husham from
the land of the Temanites reigned in his place. 35 When Husham
died, Hadad the son of Bedad, who defeated the Midianites in
the land of Moab, reigned in his place; the name of his city was
Avith. 36 When Hadad died, Samlah from Masrekah reigned in
his place. 37 When Samlah died, Shaul from Rehoboth on the
River reigned in his place. 38 When Shaul died, Baal Hanan the
son of Achbor reigned in his place. 39 When Baal Hanan the
son of Achbor died, Hadad reigned in his place; the name of his
city was Pau. His wife's name was Mehetabel, the daughter of

WEEK 3
Thursday

Genesis 36:1—37:1 (continued)

Matred, the daughter of Me-Zahab. 40 These were the names of the chiefs of Esau, according to their families, according to their places, by their names: chief Timna, chief Alvah, chief Jetheth, 41 chief Oholibamah, chief Elah, chief Pinon, 42 chief Kenaz, chief Teman, chief Mibzar, 43 chief Magdiel, chief Iram. These were the chiefs of Edom, according to their settlements in the land they possessed. This was Esau, the father of the Edomites. 37:1 But Jacob lived in the land where his father had stayed, in the land of Canaan.

Genesis 27:28–29

May God give you the dew of the sky and the richness of the earth, and plenty of grain and new wine. 29 May peoples serve you and nations bow down to you. You will be lord over your brothers, and the sons of your mother will bow down to you. May those who curse you be cursed, and those who bless you be blessed."

Genesis 27:39–40

So his father Isaac said to him, "See here, your home will be by the richness of the earth, and by the dew of the sky above. 40 You will live by your sword but you will serve your brother. When you grow restless, you will tear off his yoke from your neck."

Hebrews 10:23

And let us hold unwaveringly to the hope that we confess, for the one who made the promise is trustworthy.

Hebrews 11:20

By faith also Isaac blessed Jacob and Esau concerning the future.

SOAP

WEEK 3 • THURSDAY

SOAP / *Hebrews 10:23*
SCRIPTURE / *Write out the SOAP verses*

OBSERVATION / *Write 3 - 4 observations*

APPLICATION / *Write down 1 - 2 applications*

PRAYER / *Write out a prayer over what you learned*

SOAP

Hebrews 10:23

And let us hold unwaveringly to the hope that we confess, for the one who made the promise is trustworthy.

INTO THE TEXT

The author of Genesis gives a full account of the descendants of Abraham, focusing on those in the line of the promise while also including the records of many of Abraham's other descendants. Esau's family is recorded similarly to the way Ishmael's family is in Genesis 25.

Esau, also called Edom, took wives from among the Canaanites. Esau's choices reflect a love of the world and a continued concern for fulfilling fleshly desires. While he forgave Jacob and reconciled with his brother, Esau is described as a profane person who despised the things of God and sought worldly freedom.

While we are not given much insight into Esau's life, we can still learn from even this short account of his genealogy. Esau was the father of many chiefs and kings, ruling in the land of Edom before there were any kings in Israel. From a worldly standpoint, Esau flourished. He had many possessions and many descendants, some who were very powerful. The promise he had received from his father had indeed come to pass. Esau made his home in a prosperous area of land, lived by the sword, conquered neighboring tribes and clans, and did not submit to Jacob. The fulfillment of Esau's blessing showed the faithfulness of God. Even though Esau was not the one God had chosen, he still received a blessing.

The prosperity of Esau shows how secular greatness is often achieved much faster than spiritual greatness. It takes patience to inherit the promises of God. Often, spiritual blessings are only received after a process of refining has taken place. This was true in Jacob's life: God took him away from his home before fulfilling His promise. Yet, the blessings Esau received were another reason for Jacob to believe in God's promises. If Esau, who had not been chosen by God, still received a blessing, how much more would God fulfill the promises He had made to the one whom He had chosen?

Our God is a God of promise. He keeps all His promises in His perfect time. All of His promises are trustworthy. Most of the people we study in Genesis only saw the promise of God beginning to be fulfilled. Whether or not we can actively see God fulfilling His promises has no bearing on His ability to do so. He is the Promise-Keeper, the only One on whom we can depend. He alone is trustworthy. Let's put our faith in His promise-keeping power today.

WEEK 3
Friday

READ

Genesis 37:2–11

This is the account of Jacob. Joseph, his seventeen-year-old son, was taking care of the flocks with his brothers. Now he was a youngster working with the sons of Bilhah and Zilpah, his father's wives. Joseph brought back a bad report about them to their father. 3 Now Israel loved Joseph more than all his sons because he was a son born to him late in life, and he made a special tunic for him. 4 When Joseph's brothers saw that their father loved him more than any of them, they hated Joseph and were not able to speak to him kindly. 5 Joseph had a dream, and when he told his brothers about it they hated him even more. 6 He said to them, "Listen to this dream I had: 7 There we were, binding sheaves of grain in the middle of the field. Suddenly my sheaf rose up and stood upright and your sheaves surrounded my sheaf and bowed down to it!" 8 Then his brothers asked him, "Do you really think you will rule over us or have dominion over us?" They hated him even more because of his dream and because of what he said. 9 Then he had another dream, and told it to his brothers. "Look," he said. "I had another dream. The sun, the moon, and eleven stars were bowing down to me." 10 When he told his father and his brothers, his father rebuked him, saying, "What is this dream that you had? Will I, your mother, and your brothers really come and bow down to you?" 11 His brothers were jealous of him, but his father kept in mind what Joseph said.

Luke 16:10

"The one who is faithful in a very little is also faithful in much, and the one who is dishonest in a very little is also dishonest in much."

SOAP

WEEK 3 • FRIDAY

SOAP / *Luke 16:10*

SCRIPTURE / *Write out the SOAP verses*

OBSERVATION / *Write 3 - 4 observations*

APPLICATION / *Write down 1 - 2 applications*

PRAYER / *Write out a prayer over what you learned*

DEVOTIONAL

WEEK 3 • FRIDAY

SOAP

Luke 16:10

"The one who is faithful in a very little is also faithful in much, and the one who is dishonest in a very little is also dishonest in much."

INTO THE TEXT

The narrative of Genesis transitions to a new focus in chapter 37: the descendants of Jacob. Joseph, Jacob's eleventh son, becomes the main focus of the rest of the book. The author of Genesis uses many literary devices throughout Joseph's story to show the significance of his life as well as the continuation of God's promises.

As Joseph's story unfolds, we'll see the same themes that were present in earlier sections of Genesis: divine blessing, the use of deception, the struggle between good and evil, and prosperity and refuge in Egypt. However, Joseph is presented differently than the patriarchs. The author highlights Joseph's righteousness, faithfulness, wisdom, and patience. His character contrasts that of his father, who was known for deceitfulness and self-reliance. Presenting Joseph in this way is not meant to dishonor Jacob but is rather done to show the exemplary character of a leader who is obedient to God.

In Joseph's first recorded actions he showed responsibility, care, and faithfulness in what had been entrusted to him. His brothers, however, were unfaithful as they tended to their father's flocks, which Joseph reported to Jacob.

Though Joseph was Jacob's eleventh son, he was God's chosen leader. Joseph was faithful in a small responsibility, caring for his father's flocks. The dreams he was given showed God's calling and anointing on his life. God had appeared to Abraham, Isaac, and Jacob in dreams, confirming His choice of each of them as heir to the promise. Similarly, Joseph's dreams showed God's choice of him as the leader among his brothers.

While Joseph did not become an influential leader until much later in his life, he was faithful and obedient to God even in the little things. He was faithful when he had no authority or power, and, through these experiences, God prepared him for the future. Throughout his life Joseph was faithful, choosing the things of God over the things of the world. God did not choose him because of his righteousness, but Joseph was faithful with the calling God gave him.

We have no idea what God has planned for us. He may be preparing you now for great responsibilities in the future. He may be shaping your character to put you in a position of authority, whether in a career, in ministry, in your family, or in your church. May we choose to be faithful to Him no matter how small or insignificant our present task seems. We never know what He has in store!

REFLECT
WEEK 3

1. *Is there a relationship in your life that needs reconciliation? What is God prompting you to do as you wait for His perfect timing for the reconciliation?*

2. *Do you believe God will bring about justice? In what areas is it most difficult for you to wait on and trust in God's justice?*

3. *How will you choose to follow God today? What temptations are you facing? What is pulling you away from God and toward the things of the world?*

4. *What examples have you seen of secular greatness or success growing faster than spiritual greatness? Why do God's promises demand patience from the recipient?*

5. *Over what areas has God given you responsibility? How can you be faithful in the small things in your life? How can you be faithful in the big things God has given you?*

JOURNAL

your thoughts

JOURNAL

your thoughts

For our momentary, light suffering is producing for us an eternal weight of glory far beyond all comparison because we are not looking at what can be seen but at what cannot be seen. For what can be seen is temporary, but what cannot be seen is eternal.

2 Corinthians 4:17–18

PRAY

Write down your prayer requests and praises for this week.

WEEKLY CHALLENGE

God allowed Joseph to endure great suffering in his life to bring about His divine purposes. As you read, note Joseph's suffering. After you complete this week's reading, go back through the moments of his suffering and reflect on how God redeemed each of those events. Do you believe God can work the same way in your life? How has God already redeemed some of your seasons of suffering?

WEEK 4
Monday

READ

Genesis 37:12–26

When his brothers had gone to graze their father's flocks near Shechem, 13 Israel said to Joseph, "Your brothers are grazing the flocks near Shechem. Come, I will send you to them." "I'm ready," Joseph replied. 14 So Jacob said to him, "Go now and check on the welfare of your brothers and of the flocks, and bring me word." So Jacob sent him from the valley of Hebron. 15 When Joseph reached Shechem, a man found him wandering in the field, so the man asked him, "What are you looking for?" 16 He replied, "I'm looking for my brothers. Please tell me where they are grazing their flocks." 17 The man said, "They left this area, for I heard them say, 'Let's go to Dothan.'" So Joseph went after his brothers and found them at Dothan. 18 Now Joseph's brothers saw him from a distance, and before he reached them, they plotted to kill him. 19 They said to one another, "Here comes this master of dreams! 20 Come now, let's kill him, throw him into one of the cisterns, and then say that a wild animal ate him. Then we'll see how his dreams turn out!" 21 When Reuben heard this, he rescued Joseph from their hands, saying,"Let's not take his life!" 22 Reuben continued, "Don't shed blood! Throw him into this cistern that is here in the wilderness, but don't lay a hand on him."(Reuben said this so he could rescue Joseph from them and take him back to his father.) 23 When Joseph reached his brothers, they stripped him of his tunic, the special tunic that he wore. 24 Then they took him and threw him into the cistern. (Now the cistern was empty; there was no water in it.) 25 When they sat down to eat their food, they looked up and saw a caravan of Ishmaelites coming from Gilead. Their camels were carrying spices, balm, and myrrh down to Egypt. 26 Then Judah said to his brothers, "What profit is there if we kill our brother and cover up his blood?

WEEK 4
Monday

2 Corinthians 4:7–18

But we have this treasure in clay jars, so that the extraordinary power belongs to God and does not come from us. 8 We are experiencing trouble on every side, but are not crushed; we are perplexed, but not driven to despair; 9 we are persecuted, but not abandoned; we are knocked down, but not destroyed, 10 always carrying around in our body the death of Jesus, so that the life of Jesus may also be made visible in our body. 11 For we who are alive are constantly being handed over to death for Jesus' sake, so that the life of Jesus may also be made visible in our mortal body. 12 As a result, death is at work in us, but life is at work in you. 13 But since we have the same spirit of faith as that shown in what has been written, "***I believed; therefore I spoke***," we also believe, therefore we also speak. 14 We do so because we know that the one who raised up Jesus will also raise us up with Jesus and will bring us with you into his presence. 15 For all these things are for your sake, so that the grace that is including more and more people may cause thanksgiving to increase to the glory of God. 16 Therefore we do not despair, but even if our physical body is wearing away, our inner person is being renewed day by day. 17 For our momentary, light suffering is producing for us an eternal weight of glory far beyond all comparison 18 because we are not looking at what can be seen but at what cannot be seen. For what can be seen is temporary, but what cannot be seen is eternal.

It is incredibly gracious of God to rid us of our self-reliance.

SOAP

WEEK 4 • MONDAY

SOAP / *2 Corinthians 4:17–18*

SCRIPTURE / *Write out the SOAP verses*

OBSERVATION / *Write 3 - 4 observations*

APPLICATION / *Write down 1 - 2 applications*

PRAYER / *Write out a prayer over what you learned*

DEVOTIONAL

WEEK 4 • MONDAY

SOAP

2 Corinthians 4:17–18

For our momentary, light suffering is producing for us an eternal weight of glory far beyond all comparison because we are not looking at what can be seen but at what cannot be seen. For what can be seen is temporary, but what cannot be seen is eternal.

INTO THE TEXT

Joseph was God's chosen leader in his generation, and God revealed this calling to Joseph through dreams. Joseph was obedient to God and faithful with his responsibilities, honoring his father and doing as he was asked. At the time, Joseph was still young, about seventeen, and was living in his father's house with many of his brothers.

Jacob favored Joseph, and it caused division in his household. Because of this, Joseph's brothers hated him so much that they were unable to speak kind words to him. Though Jacob witnessed the way parental favoritism destroyed his own family relationships (see Genesis 26), he practiced the same kind of behavior and it yielded the same kind of division among his sons.

The hatred of the brothers was left unchecked and it resulted in a horrific crime. Their actions reveal the intense strife and jealousy within Jacob's family. His brothers rejected him, unaware of God's anointing on his life. The obedience and faithfulness of Joseph stands in stark contrast to the evil of his brothers as they plotted to kill him, sold him into slavery, and deceived their father.

One cannot help but notice parallels between Jacob and Joseph's stories. Jacob manipulated his brother for his birthright and then stole his blessing. Joseph's brothers attempted to destroy their brother Joseph, to whom the blessing belonged. Jacob was persecuted and deceived by Laban, and though Jacob was not innocent of deception in his actions, God saved and protected him. Joseph was persecuted by his brothers who then deceived their father, but Joseph was innocent, and God was with him just the same.

When we are faithfully serving God, we will face persecution. Those in leadership or positions of authority can be certain that they will face opposition as God's chosen leaders. Yet, even in the midst of suffering, nothing can nullify God's purposes. No amount of opposition, persecution, hardship, or suffering can alter God's plan. He protects His own, and His calling on your life cannot be altered.

WEEK 4
Tuesday

READ

Genesis 38

At that time Judah left his brothers and stayed with an Adullamite man named Hirah. 2 There Judah saw the daughter of a Canaanite man named Shua. Judah acquired her as a wife and slept with her. 3 She became pregnant and had a son. Judah named him Er. 4 She became pregnant again and had another son, whom she named Onan. 5 Then she had yet another son, whom she named Shelah. She gave birth to him in Kezib. 6 Judah acquired a wife for Er his firstborn; her name was Tamar. 7 But Er, Judah's firstborn, was evil in the LORD's sight, so the LORD killed him. 8 Then Judah said to Onan, "Sleep with your brother's wife and fulfill the duty of a brother-in-law to her so that you may raise up a descendant for your brother." 9 But Onan knew that the child would not be considered his. So whenever he slept with his brother's wife, he wasted his emission on the ground so as not to give his brother a descendant. 10 What he did was evil in the LORD's sight, so the LORD killed him too. 11 Then Judah said to his daughter-in-law Tamar, "Live as a widow in your father's house until Shelah my son grows up." For he thought, "I don't want him to die like his brothers." So Tamar went and lived in her father's house. 12 After some time Judah's wife, the daughter of Shua, died. After Judah was consoled, he left for Timnah to visit his sheep shearers, along with his friend Hirah the Adullamite. 13 Tamar was told, "Look, your father-in-law is going up to Timnah to shear his sheep." 14 So she removed her widow's clothes and covered herself with a veil. She wrapped herself and sat at the entrance to Enaim which is on the way to Timnah. (She did this because she saw that she had not been given to Shelah as a wife, even though he had now grown up.) 15 When Judah saw her, he thought she was a prostitute because she had covered her face. 16 He turned aside to her along the road and said, "Come, please, I want to sleep with you." (He did not realize it was his daughter-in-law.)

WEEK 4
Tuesday

Genesis 38 (continued)

She asked, "What will you give me so that you may sleep with
me?" 17 He replied, "I'll send you a young goat from the flock."
She asked, "Will you give me a pledge until you send it?" 18 He
said, "What pledge should I give you?" She replied, "Your seal,
your cord, and the staff that's in your hand." So he gave them
to her, then slept with her, and she became pregnant by him. 19
She left immediately, removed her veil, and put on her widow's
clothes. 20 Then Judah had his friend Hirah the Adullamite
take a young goat to get back from the woman the items he had
given in pledge, but Hirah could not find her. 21 He asked the
men who were there, "Where is the cult prostitute who was at
Enaim by the road?" But they replied, "There has been no cult
prostitute here." 22 So he returned to Judah and said, "I couldn't
find her. Moreover, the men of the place said, 'There has been
no cult prostitute here.'" 23 Judah said, "Let her keep the things
for herself. Otherwise we will appear to be dishonest. I did
indeed send this young goat, but you couldn't find her." 24 After
three months Judah was told, "Your daughter-in-law Tamar has
turned to prostitution, and as a result she has become pregnant."
Judah said, "Bring her out and let her be burned!" 25 While they
were bringing her out, she sent word to her father-in-law: "I am
pregnant by the man to whom these belong." Then she said,
"Identify the one to whom the seal, cord, and staff belong." 26
Judah recognized them and said, "She is more upright than I
am, because I wouldn't give her to Shelah my son." He was not
physically intimate with her again. 27 When it was time for her
to give birth, there were twins in her womb. 28 While she was
giving birth, one child put out his hand, and the midwife took
a scarlet thread and tied it on his hand, saying, "This one came
out first." 29 But then he drew back his hand, and his brother
came out before him. She said, "How you have broken out of the
womb!" So he was named Perez. 30 Afterward his brother came
out—the one who had the scarlet thread on his hand—and he
was named Zerah.

WEEK 4

Tuesday

Ruth 4:12

May your family become like the family of Perez—whom Tamar bore to Judah—through the descendants the LORD gives you by this young woman.

Matthew 1:2–16

Abraham was the father of Isaac, Isaac the father of Jacob, Jacob the father of Judah and his brothers, 3 Judah the father of Perez and Zerah (by Tamar), Perez the father of Hezron, Hezron the father of Ram, 4 Ram the father of Amminadab, Amminadab the father of Nahshon, Nahshon the father of Salmon, 5 Salmon the father of Boaz (by Rahab), Boaz the father of Obed (by Ruth), Obed the father of Jesse, 6 and Jesse the father of David the king. David was the father of Solomon (by the wife of Uriah), 7 Solomon the father of Rehoboam, Rehoboam the father of Abijah, Abijah the father of Asa, 8 Asa the father of Jehoshaphat, Jehoshaphat the father of Joram, Joram the father of Uzziah, 9 Uzziah the father of Jotham, Jotham the father of Ahaz, Ahaz the father of Hezekiah, 10 Hezekiah the father of Manasseh, Manasseh the father of Amon, Amon the father of Josiah, 11 and Josiah the father of Jeconiah and his brothers, at the time of the deportation to Babylon. 12 After the deportation to Babylon, Jeconiah became the father of Shealtiel, Shealtiel the father of Zerubbabel, 13 Zerubbabel the father of Abiud, Abiud the father of Eliakim, Eliakim the father of Azor, 14 Azor the father of Zadok, Zadok the father of Achim, Achim the father of Eliud, 15 Eliud the father of Eleazar, Eleazar the father of Matthan, Matthan the father of Jacob, 16 and Jacob the father of Joseph, the husband of Mary, by whom Jesus was born, who is called Christ.

SOAP

WEEK 4 • TUESDAY

SOAP / *Ruth 4:12*

SCRIPTURE / *Write out the SOAP verses*

OBSERVATION / *Write 3 - 4 observations*

APPLICATION / *Write down 1 - 2 applications*

PRAYER / *Write out a prayer over what you learned*

SOAP

Ruth 4:12

"May your family become like the family of Perez—whom Tamar bore to Judah—through the descendants the Lord *gives you by this young woman."*

INTO THE TEXT

There are consistent themes throughout the Book of Genesis, especially through the patriarchal narratives. The account of Judah and Tamar continues to display these themes, linking seemingly isolated events to the rest of the narrative.

One of these particularly evident themes is God's choice of a younger sibling over the firstborn. Judah attempted to gain the status of the firstborn by selling Joseph to the Midianites. Judah was next in line as his three elder brothers disqualified themselves through moral failure (see Genesis 34; 35:22). Though God had chosen Joseph to be the one to receive the double portion of the firstborn, Judah would also receive a blessing because of his repentance from sin and resulting obedience.

Judah betrayed and sold his brother into slavery and then deceived his father by leading him to believe Joseph was dead. He chose the things of the world, wickedness and a life far from God. He went to live with the Canaanites, the people from whom God had commanded the children of Israel to remain separate. His failure to live obediently led to the death of his sons, as they, too, were wicked before the Lord. Judah refused to give Tamar, his daughter-in-law, to his son Shelah after her husband died. God discipled Judah as He had disciplined his father. Judah deceived his father and was in turn disciplined by God through the deception of his daughter-in-law.

Tamar stands out as the only well-intended person in these events. While we may look at her actions with disdain, she was attempting to secure her future and reclaim her rights as the wife of Judah's firstborn. In the midst of a corrupt family, she kept Judah's line from assimilating with the Canaanites. She protected the family and was regarded in Israel's history with respect and honor. Her actions redeemed the line of Judah, the line through which God would bring His Son into the world.

Tamar's story shows us that no matter the desperation, no matter how far His chosen people have wandered, God is the hero. He is the one who disciplined Judah and led him back to his father's household. He is the one who brought about justice for Tamar, honoring her in Israel's history. And even in the mess of this situation, the ultimate result was the birth of the One who would save the world from sin and death. Jesus Christ descended from Judah and Tamar, reminding us that our God will always work out His good purposes, despite people's sin.

WEEK 4
Wednesday

READ

Genesis 39

Now Joseph had been brought down to Egypt. An Egyptian named Potiphar, an official of Pharaoh and the captain of the guard, purchased him from the Ishmaelites who had brought him there. 2 The LORD was with Joseph. He was successful and lived in the household of his Egyptian master. 3 His master observed that the LORD was with him and that the LORD made everything he was doing successful. 4 So Joseph found favor in his sight and became his personal attendant. Potiphar appointed Joseph overseer of his household and put him in charge of everything he owned. 5 From the time Potiphar appointed him over his household and over all that he owned, the LORD blessed the Egyptian's household for Joseph's sake. The blessing of the LORD was on everything that he had, both in his house and in his fields. 6 So Potiphar left everything he had in Joseph's care; he gave no thought to anything except the food he ate. Now Joseph was well built and good-looking. 7 Soon after these things, his master's wife took notice of Joseph and said, "Come to bed with me." 8 But he refused, saying to his master's wife, "Look, my master does not give any thought to his household with me here, and everything that he owns he has put into my care. 9 There is no one greater in this household than I am. He has withheld nothing from me except you because you are his wife. So how could I do such a great evil and sin against God?" 10 Even though she continued to speak to Joseph day after day, he did not respond to her invitation to go to bed with her. 11 One day he went into the house to do his work when none of the household servants were there in the house. 12 She grabbed him by his outer garment, saying, "Come to bed with me!" But he left his outer garment in her hand and ran outside. 13 When she saw that he had left his outer garment in her

WEEK 4
Wednesday

Genesis 39 (continued)

hand and had run outside, 14 she called for her household servants and said to them, "See, my husband brought in a Hebrew man to us to humiliate us. He tried to go to bed with me, but I screamed loudly. 15 When he heard me raise my voice and scream, he left his outer garment beside me and ran outside." 16 So she laid his outer garment beside her until his master came home. 17 This is what she said to him: "That Hebrew slave you brought to us tried to humiliate me, 18 but when I raised my voice and screamed, he left his outer garment and ran outside." 19 When his master heard his wife say, "This is the way your slave treated me," he became furious. 20 Joseph's master took him and threw him into the prison, the place where the king's prisoners were confined. So he was there in the prison. 21 But the Lord was with Joseph and showed him kindness. He granted him favor in the sight of the prison warden. 22 The warden put all the prisoners under Joseph's care. He was in charge of whatever they were doing. 23 The warden did not concern himself with anything that was in Joseph's care because the Lord was with him and whatever he was doing the Lord was making successful.

James 1:2–18

My brothers and sisters, consider it nothing but joy when you fall into all sorts of trials, 3 because you know that the testing of your faith produces endurance. 4 And let endurance have its perfect effect, so that you will be perfect and complete, not deficient in anything. 5 But if anyone

WEEK 4
Wednesday

James 1:2–18 (continued)

is deficient in wisdom, he should ask God, who gives to all generously and without reprimand, and it will be given to him. 6 But he must ask in faith without doubting, for the one who doubts is like a wave of the sea, blown and tossed around by the wind. 7 For that person must not suppose that he will receive anything from the Lord, 8 since he is a double-minded individual,unstable in all his ways. 9 Now the believer of humble means should take pride in his high position.10 But the rich person's pride should be in his humiliation, because he will pass away like a wildflower in the meadow. 11 For the sun rises with its heat and dries up the meadow; the petal of the flower falls off and its beauty is lost forever. So also the rich person in the midst of his pursuits will wither away. 12 Happy is the one who endures testing, because when he has proven to be genuine, he will receive the crown of life that God promised to those who love him. 13 Let no one say when he is tempted, "I am tempted by God," for God cannot be tempted by evil, and he himself tempts no one. 14 But each one is tempted when he is lured and enticed by his own desires. 15 Then when desire conceives, it gives birth to sin, and when sin is full grown, it gives birth to death. 16 Do not be led astray, my dear brothers and sisters. 17 All generous giving and every perfect gift is from above, coming down from the Father of lights, with whom there is no variation or the slightest hint of change. 18 By his sovereign plan he gave us birth through the message of truth, that we would be a kind of firstfruits of all he created.

SOAP

WEEK 4 • WEDNESDAY

SOAP / *James 1:12–13, 17*

SCRIPTURE / *Write out the SOAP verses*

OBSERVATION / *Write 3 - 4 observations*

APPLICATION / *Write down 1 - 2 applications*

PRAYER / *Write out a prayer over what you learned*

DEVOTIONAL

WEEK 4 • WEDNESDAY

SOAP

James 1:12–13, 17

Happy is the one who endures testing, because when he has proven to be genuine, he will receive the crown of life that God has promised to those who love him. Let no one say when he is tempted, "I am tempted by God," for God cannot be tempted by evil, and he himself tempts no one.

All generous giving and every perfect gift is from above, coming down from the Father of lights, with whom there is no variation or the slightest hint of change.

INTO THE TEXT

After chronicling the disobedience of Judah, the writer of Genesis displays the faithfulness of Joseph, God's chosen leader. The first scene in chapter 39 shows God's blessing on Joseph, confirming that His presence was with him, even in Egypt, giving him success in Potiphar's house. The focus is on God's presence and blessing, not Joseph's work. Joseph recognized God's blessing and served faithfully. Though he faced rejection and betrayal from his brothers, God brought him to a place of prominence and authority in Potiphar's house.

Joseph's dedication to God enabled him to resist temptation. Joseph was certain God had blessed him, granting success that could only come from Him. His conviction to remain faithful to God was built over time, not in his moment of temptation. Temptation came to Joseph in a time of great blessing, perhaps when he was most vulnerable, but he acted in faith and chose to obey God. His awareness of and confidence in God's presence and blessing enabled Joseph to do what honored God.

After Joseph was unfairly thrown into prison, he once again experienced God's great blessing. God continued to be with Joseph in prison the same way he was with him in Potiphar's household. Joseph's circumstances had no bearing on the faithfulness of God. Even in prison, God made Joseph successful in all he did. God rewarded Joseph's obedience, though it may not have been immediate. The renewed blessing confirmed God's calling on his life.

Joseph's example provides believers with an excellent framework of how to resist temptation. When we are not experiencing a time of testing, we must recognize that God has placed a unique calling on our lives as believers in Christ. We can successfully resist temptation if we have spent time preparing, growing in our faith and relationship with God and developing the conviction that all good things come from Him and not our own efforts. God is faithful to use trials and temptations in our lives as He prepares us for what He has planned. All blessing is from Him, and He is faithful to reward the obedience of His people in His perfect timing.

WEEK 4
Thursday

READ

Genesis 40

After these things happened, the cupbearer to the king of Egypt and the royal baker offended their master, the king of Egypt. 2 Pharaoh was enraged with his two officials, the cupbearer and the baker, 3 so he imprisoned them in the house of the captain of the guard in the same facility where Joseph was confined. 4 The captain of the guard appointed Joseph to be their attendant, and he served them. They spent some time in custody. 5 Both of them, the cupbearer and the baker of the king of Egypt, who were confined in the prison, had a dream the same night. Each man's dream had its own meaning. 6 When Joseph came to them in the morning, he saw that they were looking depressed. 7 So he asked Pharaoh's officials, who were with him in custody in his master's house, "Why do you look so sad today?" 8 They told him, "We both had dreams, but there is no one to interpret them." Joseph responded, "Don't interpretations belong to God? Tell them to me." 9 So the chief cupbearer told his dream to Joseph: "In my dream, there was a vine in front of me. 10 On the vine there were three branches. As it budded, its blossoms opened and its clusters ripened into grapes. 11 Now Pharaoh's cup was in my hand, so I took the grapes, squeezed them into his cup, and put the cup in Pharaoh's hand." 12 "This is its meaning," Joseph said to him. "The three branches represent three days. 13 In three more days Pharaoh will reinstate you and restore you to your office. You will put Pharaoh's cup in his hand, just as you did before when you were cupbearer. 14 But remember me when it goes well for you, and show me kindness. Make mention of me to Pharaoh and bring me out of this prison, 15 for I really was kidnapped from the land of the Hebrews and I have done nothing wrong here for which they should

WEEK 4
Thursday

Genesis 40 (continued)

put me in a dungeon." 16 When the chief baker saw that the interpretation of the first dream was favorable, he said to Joseph, "I also appeared in my dream and there were three baskets of white bread on my head. 17 In the top basket there were baked goods of every kind for Pharaoh, but the birds were eating them from the basket that was on my head." 18 Joseph replied, "This is its meaning: The three baskets represent three days. 19 In three more days Pharaoh will decapitate you and impale you on a pole. Then the birds will eat your flesh from you." 20 On the third day it was Pharaoh's birthday, so he gave a feast for all his servants. He "lifted up" the head of the chief cupbearer and the head of the chief baker in the midst of his servants. 21 He restored the chief cupbearer to his former position so that he placed the cup in Pharaoh's hand, 22 but the chief baker he impaled, just as Joseph had predicted. 23 But the chief cupbearer did not remember Joseph—he forgot him.

Psalm 13

How long, LORD, will you continue to ignore me? How long will you pay no attention to me? 2 How long must I worry, and suffer in broad daylight? How long will my enemy gloat over me? 3 Look at me! Answer me, O LORD my God! Revive me, or else I will die. 4 Then my enemy will say, "I have defeated him." Then my foes will rejoice because I am shaken. 5 But I trust in your faithfulness. May I rejoice because of your deliverance. 6 I will sing praises to the LORD when he vindicates me.

His justice is never misplaced, never misapplied. He is always fighting for His children.

SOAP

WEEK 4 • THURSDAY

SOAP / *Psalm 13:5–6*
SCRIPTURE / *Write out the SOAP verses*

OBSERVATION / *Write 3 - 4 observations*

APPLICATION / *Write down 1 - 2 applications*

PRAYER / *Write out a prayer over what you learned*

DEVOTIONAL

WEEK 4 • THURSDAY

SOAP

Psalm 13:5–6

But I trust in your faithfulness. May I rejoice because of your deliverance. I will sing praises to the LORD when he vindicates me.

INTO THE TEXT

In today's reading, we find Joseph at his lowest point. Joseph was the beloved son of his father, Jacob. God had given Joseph a promise of who he would become through a series of dreams, showing him that one day his brothers and father would bow to him. God had appeared to Joseph in a dream and made promises to him, just as He had done to Jacob, Isaac, and Abraham.

Since having these dreams, Joseph endured incredible hardship and injustice. His brothers betrayed him, threw him into a pit, and sold him into slavery. He found success in Potiphar's house only to be falsely accused of a crime and unfairly thrown into prison. And though Joseph rose to a position of authority in the prison, he was still living in bondage.

In all that happened to Joseph, it would be understandable if his faith faltered or if he thought he had misunderstood God's message in the first place. Yet after all these events, God gave Joseph an opportunity to demonstrate his faith, even at his lowest point.

The way the dreams of the cupbearer and baker are recorded is meant to remind the readers of Genesis of Joseph's dreams from years earlier (Genesis 37). We don't know if Joseph recognized these similarities, but the author of Genesis included these connections to show his readers how God was still at work. God had spoken to Joseph through dreams in the past, and He would continue to use dreams to tell Joseph what was to come. Joseph's thoughts are not recorded, but his actions speak volumes. By interpreting the dreams, Joseph demonstrated his unwavering faith. He still believed God spoke to His people through dreams, and he believed God would keep His promises to him.

God is working in our lives and situations. He is a God who sees, cares, and moves. We can see this in Joseph's life and find encouragement in our own circumstances. No matter what we face today, we can demonstrate our faith by continuing to believe in God's promises. God will continue to bring about His purposes; His faithfulness in the past is a model and a promise for His faithfulness in the future. He will continue to work, even when we feel we are in the pit. As the psalmist proclaimed, we can trust in His faithfulness and His coming deliverance, singing praises to Him when we are vindicated.

WEEK 4
Friday

READ

Genesis 41

At the end of two full years Pharaoh had a dream. As he was standing by the Nile, 2 seven fine-looking, fat cows were coming up out of the Nile,and they grazed in the reeds. 3 Then seven bad-looking, thin cows were coming up after them from the Nile, and they stood beside the other cows at the edge of the river. 4 The bad-looking, thin cows ate the seven fine-looking, fat cows. Then Pharaoh woke up. 5 Then he fell asleep again and had a second dream: There were seven heads of grain growing on one stalk, healthy and good. 6 Then seven heads of grain, thin and burned by the east wind, were sprouting up after them. 7 The thin heads swallowed up the seven healthy and full heads. Then Pharaoh woke up and realized it was a dream. 8 In the morning he was troubled, so he called for all the diviner-priests of Egypt and all its wise men. Pharaoh told them his dreams, but no one could interpret them for him. 9 Then the chief cupbearer said to Pharaoh, "Today I recall my failures. 10 Pharaoh was enraged with his servants, and he put me in prison in the house of the captain of the guards—me and the chief baker. 11 We each had a dream one night; each of us had a dream with its own meaning. 12 Now a young man, a Hebrew, a servant of the captain of the guards, was with us there. We told him our dreams, and he interpreted the meaning of each of our respective dreams for us. 13 It happened just as he had said to us—Pharaoh restored me to my office, but he impaled the baker." 14 Then Pharaoh summoned Joseph. So they brought him quickly out of the dungeon; he shaved himself, changed his clothes, and came before Pharaoh. 15 Pharaoh said to Joseph, "I had a dream, and there is no one who can interpret it. But I have heard about you, that you can interpret dreams." 16 Joseph replied to Pharaoh, "It is not within my power, but God will speak concerning the welfare of Pharaoh." 17 Then Pharaoh said to Joseph, "In my dream I was standing by the edge of the Nile. 18 Then seven fat and fine-looking cows were coming up out of the Nile, and they grazed in the reeds. 19 Then seven other cows came up after them; they were scrawny, very bad looking, and lean. I had never seen such bad-looking cows as these in all the land of Egypt! 20 The lean, bad-looking cows ate up the seven fat cows. 21 When they had eaten them, no one

WEEK 4
Friday

Genesis 41 (continued)

would have known that they had done so, for they were just as bad-looking as before. Then I woke up. 22 I also saw in my dream seven heads of grain growing on one stalk, full and good. 23 Then seven heads of grain, withered and thin and burned with the east wind, were sprouting up after them. 24 The thin heads of grain swallowed up the seven good heads of grain. So I told all this to the diviner-priests, but no one could tell me its meaning." 25 Then Joseph said to Pharaoh, "Both dreams of Pharaoh have the same meaning. God has revealed to Pharaoh what he is about to do. 26 The seven good cows represent seven years, and the seven good heads of grain represent seven years. Both dreams have the same meaning. 27 The seven lean, bad-looking cows that came up after them represent seven years, as do the seven empty heads of grain burned with the east wind. They represent seven years of famine. 28 This is just what I told Pharaoh: God has shown Pharaoh what he is about to do. 29 Seven years of great abundance are coming throughout the whole land of Egypt. 30 But seven years of famine will occur after them, and all the abundance will be forgotten in the land of Egypt. The famine will devastate the land. 31 The previous abundance of the land will not be remembered because of the famine that follows, for the famine will be very severe. 32 The dream was repeated to Pharaoh because the matter has been decreed by God, and God will make it happen soon. 33 "So now Pharaoh should look for a wise and discerning man and give him authority over all the land of Egypt. 34 Pharaoh should do this—he should appoint officials throughout the land to collect one-fifth of the produce of the land of Egypt during the seven years of abundance. 35 They should gather all the excess food during these good years that are coming. By Pharaoh's authority they should store up grain so the cities will have food,and they should preserve it. 36 This food should be held in storage for the land in preparation for the seven years of famine that will occur throughout the land of Egypt. In this way the land will survive the famine." 37 This advice made sense to Pharaoh and all his officials. 38 So Pharaoh asked his officials, "Can we find a man like Joseph, one in whom the Spirit of God is present?" 39 So Pharaoh said to Joseph, "Because God has enabled you to know all this, there is no one as wise and discerning as you are! 40 You will oversee my household, and all my people will

Genesis 41 (continued)

submit to your commands. Only I, the king, will be greater than
you. 41 "See here," Pharaoh said to Joseph, "I place you in authority
over all the land of Egypt." 42 Then Pharaoh took his signet ring
from his own hand and put it on Joseph's. He clothed him with fine
linen clothes and put a gold chain around his neck. 43 Pharaoh had
him ride in the chariot used by his second-in-command, and they
cried out before him, "Kneel down!" So he placed him over all the
land of Egypt. 44 Pharaoh also said to Joseph, "I am Pharaoh, but
without your permission no one will move his hand or his foot in all
the land of Egypt." 45 Pharaoh gave Joseph the name Zaphenath-
Paneah. He also gave him Asenath daughter of Potiphera, priest of
On, to be his wife. So Joseph took charge of all the land of Egypt. 46
Now Joseph was 30 years old when he began serving Pharaoh king of
Egypt. Joseph was commissioned by Pharaoh and was in charge of all
the land of Egypt. 47 During the seven years of abundance the land
produced large, bountiful harvests. 48 Joseph collected all the excess
food in the land of Egypt during the seven years and stored it in the
cities. In every city he put the food gathered from the fields around
it. 49 Joseph stored up a vast amount of grain, like the sand of the sea,
until he stopped measuring it because it was impossible to measure.
50 Two sons were born to Joseph before the famine came. Asenath
daughter of Potiphera, priest of On, was their mother. 51 Joseph
named the firstborn Manasseh, saying, "Certainly God has made me
forget all my trouble and all my father's house." 52 He named the
second child Ephraim,saying, "Certainly God has made me fruitful
in the land of my suffering." 53 The seven years of abundance in the
land of Egypt came to an end. 54 Then the seven years of famine
began, just as Joseph had predicted. There was famine in all the other
lands, but throughout the land of Egypt there was food. 55 When
all the land of Egypt experienced the famine, the people cried out
to Pharaoh for food. Pharaoh said to all the people of Egypt, "Go
to Joseph and do whatever he tells you." 56 While the famine was
over all the earth, Joseph opened the store houses and sold grain to
the Egyptians. The famine was severe throughout the land of Egypt.
57 People from every country came to Joseph in Egypt to buy grain
because the famine was severe throughout the earth.

SOAP

WEEK 4 • FRIDAY

SOAP / *Genesis 41:51–52*

SCRIPTURE / *Write out the SOAP verses*

OBSERVATION / *Write 3 - 4 observations*

APPLICATION / *Write down 1 - 2 applications*

PRAYER / *Write out a prayer over what you learned*

DEVOTIONAL

WEEK 4 • FRIDAY

SOAP

Genesis 41:51–52

Joseph named the firstborn Manasseh, saying, "Certainly God has made me forget all my trouble and all my father's house." He named the second child Ephraim, saying, "Certainly God has made me fruitful in the land of my suffering."

INTO THE TEXT

The events recorded in Genesis chapter 41 indicate a major turning point in the life of Joseph. Though he experienced great suffering, God was in control. The sovereignty of God is on display through the dreams of Pharaoh, the interpretation Joseph offered, the honor and authority given to him as a result, and the names of his children.

Joseph was thirty years old when he began serving Pharaoh in Egypt; he was seventeen when his brothers sold him to the Midianites. Joseph spent at least two of those thirteen years in prison, likely many more. Yet, even though he faced great injustice and suffering, Joseph remained faithful to God, seeking Him and walking in obedience no matter his circumstances.

God displayed His sovereignty over the nations by revealing His plans to bless the Egyptians with an abundant harvest and then humble them with a great famine. God controls everything, from nature to the most powerful nations and rulers. And when this powerful nation could not interpret the plans of God, He restored His faithful servant to a place of honor as He brought about His sovereign plans.

In revealing His plans for Egypt, God also revealed His specific plans for Joseph, His chosen leader. God, not Pharaoh, appointed Joseph to be in charge of the nation of Egypt at this time. Joseph's faithfulness in the little things was honored and he was put in charge of many things (Genesis 37:2; 39:1–6, 21–23). Finally, after much heartache and suffering, Joseph could see God's wonderful plan for him unfolding before his eyes.

The names of Joseph's sons display his gratitude for and recognition of what God had done in his life. The name Manasseh was a reminder that God allowed Joseph to forget his trouble and his father's house. Ephraim's name was a reminder that God allowed Joseph to be fruitful in the land of his suffering. Joseph recognized God's provision and care over his life. He acknowledged God's work and deliverance for him, and his children's names were permanent reminders of God's faithfulness.

Joseph consistently chose the things of God. He was faithful in everything God had given him, from his father's flocks to Potiphar's house, from the prisoners to the entire nation of Egypt. His faithfulness is a model for followers of Christ. No matter where we are, we can remain faithful and obedient to God. While it may not be immediate, God will one day reward those who are devoted to Him.

REFLECT
WEEK 4

1. *Do you have to endure hardship as a leader, like Joseph? Or are you, like his brothers, tempted to oppose those God has chosen as leaders over you? How can you maintain an eternal mindset in these situations?*

2. *Have you faced a situation where you have felt the need to resort to desperate means to bring about God's purposes? How can you remain obedient to God even in a difficult situation? How can you trust Him today, even if you are in the middle of a mess?*

3. *How can you prepare today to resist temptation in the future?*

4. *How was God's faithfulness shown to Joseph in prison? How have you seen God show His faithfulness to you when you were in a season of despair?*

5. *When has God been faithful to redeem you from a season of suffering? If you are enduring a season of suffering now, what can you do today to remind yourself of His faithfulness?*

JOURNAL

your thoughts

JOURNAL

your thoughts

Finally, all of you be harmonious, sympathetic, affectionate, compassionate, and humble. Do not return evil for evil or insult for insult, but instead bless others because you were called to inherit a blessing.

1 Peter 3:8-9

PRAY

Write down your prayer requests and praises for this week.

WEEKLY CHALLENGE

This week we will focus on Joseph's process of testing his brothers, as well as their reconciliation. Is there someone with whom you need to reconcile? Take steps to forgive them first, and then, if possible, seek reconciliation. Record how God works in your life and how you see His faithfulness in the process.

WEEK 5
Monday

READ

Genesis 42

When Jacob heard there was grain in Egypt, he said to his sons, "Why are you looking at each other?" 2 He then said, "Look, I hear that there is grain in Egypt. Go down there and buy grain for us so that we may live and not die." 3 So ten of Joseph's brothers went down to buy grain from Egypt. 4 But Jacob did not send Joseph's brother Benjamin with his brothers, for he said, "What if some accident happens to him?" 5 So Israel's sons came to buy grain among the other travelers, for the famine was severe in the land of Canaan. 6 Now Joseph was the ruler of the country, the one who sold grain to all the people of the country. Joseph's brothers came and bowed down before him with their faces to the ground. 7 When Joseph saw his brothers, he recognized them, but he pretended to be a stranger to them and spoke to them harshly. He asked, "Where do you come from?" They answered, "From the land of Canaan, to buy grain for food." 8 Joseph recognized his brothers, but they did not recognize him. 9 Then Joseph remembered the dreams he had dreamed about them, and he said to them, "You are spies; you have come to see if our land is vulnerable!" 10 But they exclaimed, "No, my lord! Your servants have come to buy grain for food! 11 We are all the sons of one man; we are honest men! Your servants are not spies." 12 "No," he insisted, "but you have come to see if our land is vulnerable." 13 They replied, "Your servants are from a family of twelve brothers. We are the sons of one man in the land of Canaan. The youngest is with our father at this time, and one is no longer alive." 14 But Joseph told them, "It is just as I said to you: You are spies! 15 You will be tested in this way: As surely as Pharaoh lives, you will not depart from this place unless your youngest brother comes here. 16 One of you must

WEEK 5
Monday

Genesis 42 (continued)

go and get your brother, while the rest of you remain in prison. In this way your words may be tested to see if you are telling the truth. If not, then, as surely as Pharaoh lives, you are spies!" 17 He imprisoned them all for three days. 18 On the third day Joseph said to them, "Do as I say and you will live, for I fear God. 19 If you are honest men, leave one of your brothers confined here in prison while the rest of you go and take grain back for your hungry families. 20 But you must bring your youngest brother to me. Then your words will be verified and you will not die." They did as he said. 21 They said to one another, "Surely we're being punished because of our brother, because we saw how distressed he was when he cried to us for mercy, but we refused to listen. That is why this distress has come on us!" 22 Reuben said to them, "Didn't I say to you, 'Don't sin against the boy,' but you wouldn't listen? So now we must pay for shedding his blood!" 23 (Now they did not know that Joseph could understand them, for he was speaking through an interpreter.) 24 He turned away from them and wept. When he turned around and spoke to them again, he had Simeon taken from them and tied up before their eyes. 25 Then Joseph gave orders to fill their bags with grain, to return each man's money to his sack, and to give them provisions for the journey. His orders were carried out. 26 So they loaded their grain on their donkeys and left. 27 When one of them opened his sack to get feed for his donkey at their resting place, he saw his money in the mouth of his sack. 28 He said to his brothers, "My money was returned! Here it is in my sack!" They were dismayed; they turned trembling to one another and said, "What in the world has God done to us?" 29 They returned to their father Jacob in the land of Canaan and told him all the things that had happened to them, saying, 30 "The man, the lord of the land, spoke harshly to us and treated us

WEEK 5
Monday

Genesis 42 (continued)

as if we were spying on the land. 31 But we said to him, 'We are honest men; we are not spies! 32 We are from a family of twelve brothers; we are the sons of one father. One is no longer alive, and the youngest is with our father at this time in the land of Canaan.' 33 "Then the man, the lord of the land, said to us, 'This is how I will find out if you are honest men. Leave one of your brothers with me, and take grain for your hungry households and go. 34 But bring your youngest brother back to me so I will know that you are honest men and not spies. Then I will give your brother back to you and you may move about freely in the land.'" 35 When they were emptying their sacks, there was each man's bag of money in his sack! When they and their father saw the bags of money, they were afraid. 36 Their father Jacob said to them, "You are making me childless! Joseph is gone. Simeon is gone. And now you want to take Benjamin! Everything is against me." 37 Then Reuben said to his father, "You may put my two sons to death if I do not bring him back to you. Put him in my care and I will bring him back to you." 38 But Jacob replied, "My son will not go down there with you, for his brother is dead and he alone is left. If an accident happens to him on the journey you have to make, then you will bring down my gray hair in sorrow to the grave."

2 Corinthians 7:9–10

Now I rejoice, not because you were made sad, but because you were made sad to the point of repentance. For you were made sad as God intended, so that you were not harmed in any way by us. 10 For sadness as intended by God produces a repentance that leads to salvation, leaving no regret, but worldly sadness brings about death.

SOAP

WEEK 5 • MONDAY

SOAP / *2 Corinthians 7:9–10*

SCRIPTURE / *Write out the SOAP verses*

OBSERVATION / *Write 3 - 4 observations*

APPLICATION / *Write down 1 - 2 applications*

PRAYER / *Write out a prayer over what you learned*

SOAP

2 Corinthians 7:9–10

Now I rejoice, not because you were made sad, but because you were made sad to the point of repentance. For you were made sad as God intended, so that you were not harmed in any way by us. For sadness as intended by God produces a repentance that leads to salvation, leaving no regret, but worldly sadness brings about death.

INTO THE TEXT

Jacob and his family, living in the land of Canaan, ran out of food and were desperate for grain. Once again, Egypt was a place of refuge for God's people: Abraham sought refuge in Egypt when he experienced a famine (Genesis 12:10); Isaac intended to go to Egypt during a famine, but God instructed him otherwise (Genesis 26:1–3); Joseph found refuge from the suffering of his father's household in Egypt (Genesis 41:51); and, centuries later, Egypt would be the place of refuge for Jesus and his parents as they escaped the wrath of Herod (Matthew 2:13–16).

When Joseph's brothers arrived in Egypt, he immediately recognized them. Joseph's dream came true before his eyes when his brothers bowed to him as the ruler of the country. Joseph put his brothers through a series of tests to determine if they felt any remorse for their crimes against him. The brothers, as heirs of God's promise, needed to prove faithful to become God's chosen nation. They needed to acknowledge their guilt and recognize the discipline of God, proving they were repentant and changed. God used this encounter to awaken their consciences and turn their hearts back to Him.

Reuben's declaration of guilt in Egypt and his vow to Jacob after returning to Canaan is a representation of the brothers' repentance. He displayed a changed heart and repentance from past sin. Reuben's actions represent how the brothers' hearts had changed and returned to the things of God. He was willing to make sacrifices (though possibly foolish ones) to redeem and restore the family of Jacob. Jacob's sons would become the fathers of God's chosen nation because they acknowledged their guilt, repented, and then acted righteously.

Can we be trusted to act righteously when God reveals our guilt? Will we choose the things of God—repentance and humility—or will we act pridefully or defensively? In his letter to the church in Corinth, Paul explained how sadness is sometimes intended by God to bring us to repentance. This repentance is what brings us to acknowledge our need for a Savior, place our faith in Christ, and receive eternal life in Him. May we recognize sadness over sin as coming from God and be faithful to repent.

WEEK 5
Tuesday

READ

Genesis 43

Now the famine was severe in the land. 2 When they finished eating the grain they had brought from Egypt, their father said to them, "Return, buy us a little more food." 3 But Judah said to him, "The man solemnly warned us, 'You will not see my face unless your brother is with you.' 4 If you send our brother with us, we'll go down and buy food for you. 5 But if you will not send him, we won't go down there because the man said to us, 'You will not see my face unless your brother is with you.'" 6 Israel said, "Why did you bring this trouble on me by telling the man you had one more brother?" 7 They replied, "The man questioned us thoroughly about ourselves and our family, saying, 'Is your father still alive? Do you have another brother?' So we answered him in this way. How could we possibly know that he would say, 'Bring your brother down'?" 8 Then Judah said to his father Israel, "Send the boy with me and we will go immediately. Then we will live and not die—we and you and our little ones. 9 I myself pledge security for him; you may hold me liable. If I do not bring him back to you and place him here before you, I will bear the blame before you all my life. 10 But if we had not delayed, we could have traveled there and back twice by now!" 11 Then their father Israel said to them, "If it must be so, then do this: Take some of the best products of the land in your bags, and take a gift down to the man—a little balm and a little honey, spices and myrrh, pistachios and almonds. 12 Take double the money with you; you must take back the money that was returned in the mouths of your sacks—perhaps it was an oversight. 13 Take your brother too, and go right away to the man. 14 May the Sovereign God grant you mercy before the man so that he may release your other brother

WEEK 5
Tuesday

Genesis 43 (continued)

and Benjamin! As for me, if I lose my children I lose them."
15 So the men took these gifts, and they took double the
money with them, along with Benjamin. Then they hurried
down to Egypt and stood before Joseph. 16 When Joseph
saw Benjamin with them, he said to the servant who was
over his household, "Bring the men to the house. Slaughter
an animal and prepare it, for the men will eat with me at
noon." 17 The man did just as Joseph said; he brought the
men into Joseph's house. 18 But the men were afraid when
they were brought to Joseph's house. They said, "We are
being brought in because of the money that was returned
in our sacks last time. He wants to capture us,make us
slaves, and take our donkeys!" 19 So they approached the
man who was in charge of Joseph's household and spoke to
him at the entrance to the house. 20 They said, "My lord,
we did indeed come down the first time to buy food. 21
But when we came to the place where we spent the night,
we opened our sacks and each of us found his money—
the full amount—in the mouth of his sack. So we have
returned it. 22 We have brought additional money with
us to buy food. We do not know who put the money in
our sacks!" 23 "Everything is fine," the man in charge of
Joseph's household told them. "Don't be afraid. Your God
and the God of your father has given you treasure in your
sacks. I had your money." Then he brought Simeon out
to them. 24 The servant in charge brought the men into
Joseph's house. He gave them water, and they washed their
feet. Then he gave food to their donkeys. 25 They got their
gifts ready for Joseph's arrival at noon, for they had heard
that they were to have a meal there. 26 When Joseph came
home, they presented him with the gifts they had brought

WEEK 5
Tuesday

Genesis 43 (continued)

inside, and they bowed down to the ground before him.
27 He asked them how they were doing. Then he said,
"Is your aging father well, the one you spoke about? Is
he still alive?" 28 "Your servant our father is well," they
replied. "He is still alive." They bowed down in humility.
29 When Joseph looked up and saw his brother Benjamin,
his mother's son, he said, "Is this your youngest brother,
whom you told me about?" Then he said, "May God be
gracious to you, my son." 30 Joseph hurried out, for he was
overcome by affection for his brother and was at the point
of tears. So he went to his room and wept there. 31 Then he
washed his face and came out. With composure he said,"Set
out the food." 32 They set a place for him, a separate place
for his brothers, and another for the Egyptians who were
eating with him. (The Egyptians are not able to eat with
Hebrews, for the Egyptians think it is disgusting to do
so.) 33 They sat before him, arranged by order of birth,
beginning with the firstborn and ending with the youngest.
The men looked at each other in astonishment. 34 He gave
them portions of the food set before him, but the portion
for Benjamin was five times greater than the portions for
any of the others. They drank with Joseph until they all
became drunk.

1 Peter 3:8–9

Finally, all of you be harmonious, sympathetic, affectionate,
compassionate, and humble. 9 Do not return evil for evil or
insult for insult, but instead bless others because you were
called to inherit a blessing.

SOAP

WEEK 5 • TUESDAY

SOAP / *1 Peter 3:8–9*

SCRIPTURE / *Write out the SOAP verses*

OBSERVATION / *Write 3 - 4 observations*

APPLICATION / *Write down 1 - 2 applications*

PRAYER / *Write out a prayer over what you learned*

DEVOTIONAL

WEEK 5 • TUESDAY

SOAP

1 Peter 3:8–9

Finally, all of you be harmonious, sympathetic, affectionate, compassionate, and humble. Do not return evil for evil or insult for insult, but instead bless others because you were called to inherit a blessing.

INTO THE TEXT

On their first visit to Egypt, the brothers recognized their guilt and were remorseful over the way they treated Joseph, even though they had no idea they were facing him again. On their second visit, Joseph presented them with another test.

The favoritism of Joseph by their father had led to the brothers' actions against him. In this test, Joseph favored Benjamin by giving him a greater portion of food. This presented the brothers with an opportunity to leave Benjamin behind and betray him like they had Joseph. By testing his brothers in this way Joseph could see if their hearts had truly changed or if they would still act selfishly and maliciously when one of Rachel's sons was favored.

Joseph's brothers showed great maturity and a radical change of heart. God worked in them through His mercy, provision, and grace. Judah's promise to Jacob, their willingness to pay back the cost of grain to the Egyptians, their enjoyment of the feast despite the favoritism shown to Benjamin, and their awareness of God's intervention all displayed the brothers' proper response to testing.

The Book of Genesis was written to the generation of Israelites preparing to enter the Promised Land of Canaan. The brothers presented a model to the nation of Israel (and the church today) of how to live as a recipient of God's blessing. They displayed responsibility in their vow to care for Benjamin, honesty in their willingness to pay for what they purchased, unity in their efforts to return to Egypt to rescue Simeon, faith in their recognition of God's intervention, and gratitude in their enjoyment of the feast without jealousy. God alone had changed their hearts as He prepared them to bring their families to Egypt and become His chosen nation.

Believers in Christ are called to develop these same attributes as we build up and bless the body of Christ. Like the nation of Israel, we are called to inherit a blessing through Christ. As we seek to represent Him to the world, may we develop responsibility, honesty, unity, faith, and gratitude. May we recognize God's mercy, provision, and grace in all things, allowing Him to mature us so that we may prove faithful in times of testing.

WEEK 5
Wednesday

READ

Genesis 44

He instructed the servant who was over his household, "Fill the sacks of the men with as much food as they can carry and put each man's money in the mouth of his sack. 2 Then put my cup—the silver cup—in the mouth of the youngest one's sack, along with the money for his grain." He did as Joseph instructed. 3 When morning came, the men and their donkeys were sent off. 4 They had not gone very far from the city when Joseph said to the servant who was over his household, "Pursue the men at once! When you overtake them, say to them, 'Why have you repaid good with evil? 5 Doesn't my master drink from this cup and use it for divination? You have done wrong!'" 6 When the man overtook them, he spoke these words to them. 7 They answered him, "Why does my lord say such things? Far be it from your servants to do such a thing! 8 Look, the money that we found in the mouths of our sacks we brought back to you from the land of Canaan. Why then would we steal silver or gold from your master's house? 9 If one of us has it, he will die, and the rest of us will become my lord's slaves!" 10 He replied, "You have suggested your own punishment! The one who has it will become my slave, but the rest of you will go free."11 So each man quickly lowered his sack to the ground and opened it. 12 Then the man searched. He began with the oldest and finished with the youngest. The cup was found in Benjamin's sack! 13 They all tore their clothes! Then each man loaded his donkey, and they returned to the city. 14 So Judah and his brothers came back to Joseph's house. He was still there, and they threw themselves to the ground before him. 15 Joseph said to them, "What did you think you were doing? Don't you know that a man like me can find out things like this by divination?" 16 Judah replied, "What can we say to my

WEEK 5
Wednesday

Genesis 44 (continued)

lord? What can we speak? How can we clear ourselves? God has exposed the sin of your servants! We are now my lord's slaves, we and the one in whose possession the cup was
found." 17 But Joseph said, "Far be it from me to do this! The man in whose hand the cup was found will become my slave, but the rest of you may go back to your father
in peace." 18 Then Judah approached him and said, "My lord, please allow your servant to speak a word with you. Please do not get angry with your servant, for you are just
like Pharaoh. 19 My lord asked his servants, 'Do you have
a father or a brother?' 20 We said to my lord, 'We have an aged father, and there is a young boy who was born when our father was old. The boy's brother is dead. He is the only one of his mother's sons left, and his father loves him.'
21 "Then you told your servants, 'Bring him down to me
so I can see him.' 22 We said to my lord, 'The boy cannot leave his father. If he leaves his father, his father will die.'
23 But you said to your servants, 'If your youngest brother does not come down with you, you will not see my face
again.' 24 When we returned to your servant my father, we
told him the words of my lord. 25 "Then our father said,
'Go back and buy us a little food.' 26 But we replied, 'We cannot go down there. If our youngest brother is with us, then we will go, for we won't be permitted to see the man's
face if our youngest brother is not with us.' 27 "Then your servant my father said to us, 'You know that my wife gave
me two sons. 28 The first disappeared and I said, "He has
surely been torn to pieces." I have not seen him since. 29 If you take this one from me too and an accident happens to him, then you will bring down my gray hair in tragedy to
the grave.' 30 "So now, when I return to your servant my

Genesis 44 (continued)

father, and the boy is not with us—his very life is bound up
in his son's life. 31 When he sees the boy is not with us, he
will die, and your servants will bring down the gray hair of
your servant our father in sorrow to the grave. 32 Indeed,
your servant pledged security for the boy with my father,
saying, 'If I do not bring him back to you, then I will bear
the blame before my father all my life.' 33 "So now, please
let your servant remain as my lord's slave instead of the boy.
As for the boy, let him go back with his brothers. 34 For
how can I go back to my father if the boy is not with me? I
couldn't bear to see my father's pain."

John 15:12–13

My commandment is this—to love one another just as I
have loved you. 13 No one has greater love than this—that
one lays down his life for his friends.

1 John 1:8—2:2

If we say we do not bear the guilt of sin, we are deceiving
ourselves and the truth is not in us. 9 But if we confess our
sins, he is faithful and righteous, forgiving us our sins and
cleansing us from all unrighteousness. 10 If we say we have
not sinned, we make him a liar and his word is not in us.
2:1 (My little children, I am writing these things to you so
that you may not sin.) But if anyone does sin, we have an
advocate with the Father, Jesus Christ the Righteous One, 2
and he himself is the atoning sacrifice for our sins, and not
only for our sins but also for the whole world.

SOAP

WEEK 5 • WEDNESDAY

SOAP / *John 15:12–13*
SCRIPTURE / *Write out the SOAP verses*

OBSERVATION / *Write 3 - 4 observations*

APPLICATION / *Write down 1 - 2 applications*

PRAYER / *Write out a prayer over what you learned*

SOAP

John 15:12–13

"My commandment is this—to love one another just as I have loved you. No one has greater love than this—that one lays down his life for his friends."

INTO THE TEXT

After feasting with his brothers, Joseph put them through one final test by falsely accusing them of theft. He tested them to see if they would value Benjamin's life more than their own, something they had not done for Joseph. More than twenty years had passed since Judah suggested selling Joseph to a band of Ishmaelites. And surprisingly enough, Judah was the one willing to sacrifice himself to save Benjamin.

They had been found out. Though they had not committed the crime they were accused of, Judah acknowledged their crimes against Joseph, recognizing how God had exposed their sin after all. They were accused of what they had not done in order for them to acknowledge what they had done. Judah gave Joseph's life away, trading him for twenty pieces of silver. However, Judah displayed a changed heart as he offered himself in Benjamin's place.

God restored the unity of His chosen family through these events. Judah's willingness to sacrifice himself showed he was fit for leadership in God's nation—the greatest kings of God's people would come from his line. His actions represented a willingness to protect his family and maintain unity, unity that could only be restored if someone was ready to endure suffering on behalf of his brother.

Generations later, a descendant of Judah would perform the greatest act of sacrificial love by offering Himself for the sins of others. He endured suffering so we could be saved.

As humans, we have all sinned, all chosen to rebel against and disobey God's commands. Because of this, our unity with Him was broken. But, like Joseph's family, our unity with God is restored because of the willingness of one to suffer on behalf of others. Jesus Christ offered Himself for us, suffering the consequences of sin so we could be restored to God. His sacrifice is the ultimate display of love and unity.

Only by acknowledging our sin before God, can we be restored to unity with Him. If we say we have no sin, we are only deceiving ourselves and keeping ourselves from a life of freedom in Christ. When we confess our sins, He is faithful to forgive us and restore our relationship with God the Father. He is our advocate, our means of unity with the Father because He laid down His life for us. His love is unmatched!

WEEK 5

Thursday

READ

Genesis 45:1–15

Joseph was no longer able to control himself before all his attendants, so he cried out, "Make everyone go out from my presence!" No one remained with Joseph when he made himself known to his brothers. 2 He wept loudly; the Egyptians heard it and Pharaoh's household heard about it. 3 Joseph said to his brothers, "I am Joseph! Is my father still alive?" His brothers could not answer him because they were dumbfounded before him. 4 Joseph said to his brothers, "Come closer to me," so they came near. Then he said, "I am Joseph your brother, whom you sold into Egypt. 5 Now, do not be upset and do not be angry with yourselves because you sold me here, for God sent me ahead of you to preserve life! 6 For these past two years there has been famine in the land and for five more years there will be neither plowing nor harvesting. 7 God sent me ahead of you to preserve you on the earth and to save your lives by a great deliverance. 8 So now, it is not you who sent me here, but God. He has made me an adviser to Pharaoh, lord over all his household, and ruler over all the land of Egypt. 9 Now go up to my father quickly and tell him, 'This is what your son Joseph says: "God has made me lord of all Egypt. Come down to me; do not delay! 10 You will live in the land of Goshen, and you will be near me—you, your children, your grandchildren, your flocks, your herds, and everything you have. 11 I will provide you with food there because there will be five more years of famine. Otherwise you would become poor—you, your household, and everyone who belongs to you."' 12 You and my brother Benjamin can certainly see with your own eyes that I really am the one who speaks to you. 13 So tell my father about all my honor in Egypt and about everything you have seen. But bring my father down here quickly!" 14 Then he threw himself on the neck of his brother Benjamin and wept, and Benjamin wept on his neck. 15 He kissed all his brothers and wept over them. After this his brothers talked with him.

SOAP

WEEK 5 • THURSDAY

SOAP / *Genesis 45:5*

SCRIPTURE / *Write out the SOAP verses*

OBSERVATION / *Write 3 - 4 observations*

APPLICATION / *Write down 1 - 2 applications*

PRAYER / *Write out a prayer over what you learned*

DEVOTIONAL

WEEK 5 • THURSDAY

SOAP

Genesis 45:5

"Now, do not be upset and do not be angry with yourselves because you sold me here, for God sent me ahead of you to preserve life!"

INTO THE TEXT

The message of reconciliation is a common theme in the Book of Genesis. When Jacob prepared to meet Esau after twenty years apart, he was greatly concerned. Esau, however, had forgiven Jacob for his deception because he had also been abundantly blessed (Genesis 33:9). Similarly, Joseph's brothers were concerned that they would face severe punishment for the wrongs they had done to Joseph. Instead, Joseph offered them forgiveness and sought reconciliation. He was able to do so because of his understanding of God's sovereignty.

Instead of retaliating or punishing his brothers when they acknowledged their guilt, Joseph forgave them. He realized that even though his brothers sold him into slavery, it was God who sent him there. God worked amazing things in the two decades since the incident, using all the wrongs against Joseph for good. Joseph recognized God's sovereignty and did not need to seek revenge.

A proper understanding of God's sovereignty leads to forgiveness. Joseph saw how God used the wrongs against him to bring about a greater good and to preserve the lives of his family members. Instead of responding in retaliation, Joseph responded with compassion. His compassion, in turn, led to reconciliation between the brothers. The unity of the family was restored.

God is always working. These events display His desire to preserve life and His ability to use even evil to bring about His sovereign purposes. God includes all things in His plan, and because of this, there should be no room in our hearts for retaliation or bitterness.

True reconciliation can only come from God's work in us. Without forgiveness, reconciliation is impossible. But without a proper understanding and acknowledgment of God's sovereignty, we will be unwilling to forgive those who have wronged us. Holding a grudge or seeking retaliation displays an unwillingness or inability to accept the sovereignty of God. He is working in all things, even evil, to bring about His purposes. When we view the events in our lives as pieces of God's grand plan of redemption, we can, with His help, forgive others and be reconciled to them.

What a blessing this account of the brothers is to us as we strive for unity with other believers. If Joseph was able to forgive his brothers, surely we can surrender our need for retaliation and instead seek reconciliation with other believers. Unity was crucial in the chosen family of God, and it is just as crucial in the body of Christ today.

WEEK 5
Friday

READ

Genesis 45:16—46:30

Now it was reported in the household of Pharaoh, "Joseph's brothers have arrived." It pleased Pharaoh and his servants. 17 Pharaoh said to Joseph, "Say to your brothers, 'Do this: Load your animals and go to the land of Canaan! 18 Get your father and your households and come to me! Then I will give you the best land in Egypt and you will eat the best of the land.' 19 You are also commanded to say, 'Do this: Take for yourselves wagons from the land of Egypt for your little ones and for your wives. Bring your father and come. 20 Don't worry about your belongings, for the best of all the land of Egypt will be yours.'" 21 So the sons of Israel did as he said. Joseph gave them wagons as Pharaoh had instructed, and he gave them provisions for the journey. 22 He gave sets of clothes to each one of them, but to Benjamin he gave 300 pieces of silver and five sets of clothes. 23 To his father he sent the following: ten donkeys loaded with the best products of Egypt and ten female donkeys loaded with grain, food, and provisions for his father's journey. 24 Then he sent his brothers on their way and they left. He said to them, "As you travel don't be overcome with fear." 25 So they went up from Egypt and came to their father Jacob in the land of Canaan. 26 They told him, "Joseph is still alive and he is ruler over all the land of Egypt!" Jacob was stunned, for he did not believe them. 27 But when they related to him everything Joseph had said to them, and when he saw the wagons that Joseph had sent to transport him, their father Jacob's spirit revived. 28 Then Israel said, "Enough! My son Joseph is still alive! I will go and see him before I die." 46:1 So Israel began his journey, taking with him all that he had. When he came to Beer Sheba he offered sacrifices to the God of his father Isaac. 2 God spoke to

WEEK 5
Friday

Genesis 45:16—46:30 (continued)

Israel in a vision during the night and said, "Jacob, Jacob!"
He replied, "Here I am!" 3 He said, "I am God, the God
of your father. Do not be afraid to go down to Egypt, for
I will make you into a great nation there. 4 I will go down
with you to Egypt and I myself will certainly bring you
back from there. Joseph will close your eyes." 5 Then Jacob
started out from Beer Sheba, and the sons of Israel carried
their father Jacob, their little children, and their wives in
the wagons that Pharaoh had sent along to transport him.
6 Jacob and all his descendants took their livestock and the
possessions they had acquired in the land of Canaan, and
they went to Egypt. 7 He brought with him to Egypt his
sons and grandsons, his daughters and granddaughters—
all his descendants. 8 These are the names of the sons of
Israel who went to Egypt—Jacob and his sons: Reuben, the
firstborn of Jacob. 9 The sons of Reuben: Hanoch, Pallu,
Hezron, and Carmi. 10 The sons of Simeon: Jemuel, Jamin,
Ohad, Jakin, Zohar, and Shaul (the son of a Canaanite
woman). 11 The sons of Levi: Gershon, Kohath, and
Merari. 12 The sons of Judah: Er, Onan, Shelah, Perez,
and Zerah (but Er and Onan died in the land of Canaan).
The sons of Perez were Hezron and Hamul. 13 The sons of
Issachar: Tola, Puah, Jashub, and Shimron. 14 The sons of
Zebulun: Sered, Elon, and Jahleel. 15 These were the sons
of Leah, whom she bore to Jacob in Paddan Aram, along
with Dinah his daughter. His sons and daughters numbered
thirty-three in all. 16 The sons of Gad: Zephon, Haggi,

WEEK 5
Friday

Genesis 45:16—46:30 (continued)

Shuni, Ezbon, Eri, Arodi, and Areli. 17 The sons of Asher:
Imnah, Ishvah, Ishvi, Beriah, and Serah their sister. The
sons of Beriah were Heber and Malkiel. 18 These were the
sons of Zilpah, whom Laban gave to Leah his daughter. She
bore these to Jacob, sixteen in all. 19 The sons of Rachel
the wife of Jacob: Joseph and Benjamin. 20 Manasseh and
Ephraim were born to Joseph in the land of Egypt. Asenath
daughter of Potiphera, priest of On, bore them to him. 21
The sons of Benjamin: Bela, Beker, Ashbel, Gera, Naaman,
Ehi, Rosh, Muppim, Huppim and Ard. 22 These were the
sons of Rachel who were born to Jacob, fourteen in all. 23
The son of Dan: Hushim. 24 The sons of Naphtali: Jahziel,
Guni, Jezer, and Shillem. 25 These were the sons of Bilhah,
whom Laban gave to Rachel his daughter. She bore these to
Jacob, seven in all. 26 All the direct descendants of Jacob
who went to Egypt with him were sixty-six in number.
(This number does not include the wives of Jacob's sons.)
27 Counting the two sons of Joseph who were born to him
in Egypt, all the people of the household of Jacob who were
in Egypt numbered seventy. 28 Jacob sent Judah before him
to Joseph to accompany him to Goshen. So they came to
the land of Goshen. 29 Joseph harnessed his chariot and
went up to meet his father Israel in Goshen. When he met
him, he hugged his neck and wept on his neck for quite
some time. 30 Israel said to Joseph, "Now let me die since I
have seen your face and know that you are still alive."

SOAP

WEEK 5 • FRIDAY

SOAP / *Genesis 46:2–4*

SCRIPTURE / *Write out the SOAP verses*

OBSERVATION / *Write 3 - 4 observations*

APPLICATION / *Write down 1 - 2 applications*

PRAYER / *Write out a prayer over what you learned*

DEVOTIONAL

WEEK 5 • FRIDAY

SOAP

Genesis 46:2–4

God spoke to Israel in a vision during the night and said, "Jacob, Jacob!" He replied, "Here I am!" He said, "I am God, the God of your father. Do not be afraid to go down to Egypt, for I will make you into a great nation there. I will go down with you to Egypt and I myself will certainly bring you back from there. Joseph will close your eyes."

INTO THE TEXT

The Book of Genesis chronicles the beginnings of a family through whom God would bless the world. This family began with a man named Abram (later Abraham). God promised to give him many descendants, to provide them with a land of their own, and through them bless all the nations of the earth. God also told Abram that his descendants would be strangers in a foreign country, where they would eventually be enslaved and oppressed, but that He would deliver them from their enemy in His perfect time (Genesis 15:13–16).

This promise passed from Abraham to his son Isaac, and from Isaac to his son Jacob. Though the last several chapters of Genesis have focused primarily on Jacob's son Joseph, in today's reading we discover that the events are recorded to show how God brought Jacob and his family (descendants of Abraham) to the foreign land of Egypt.

This account connects the narrative to the patriarchal promises earlier in the book, reminding the readers of Genesis of God's faithfulness and sovereignty. The plans He revealed to Abram were never set aside. He was working through His chosen people and in His perfect timing to bring about His ultimate plan.

God had previously appeared to Jacob in dreams at significant moments in his life: at Bethel, confirming His calling on Jacob's life (Genesis 28:10–22), and in Paddan Aram, when God instructed him to return to the land of his fathers (Genesis 31:1–3). And, once again, God appeared to Jacob in a dream to give him instructions and confirm His promises as he was on his way to Egypt. In Egypt, God would continue to build Jacob's family into a great nation. He also promised to bring Jacob's family out of Egypt and back into the land He promised to give them.

God may lead us to places we don't expect or present us with circumstances we do not understand. In these moments, we can depend on the promise-keeping character of our God. He is the one who makes the promise, and He is the one who is faithful to keep it. May we cling to His promises and trust His timing and His character, no matter what.

REFLECT
WEEK 5

1. *How does sadness lead to repentance and salvation? Have you experienced the sadness of God? Did it lead you to repentance?*

2. *How can you develop responsibility, honesty, unity, faith, and gratitude? How do these characteristics bless the body of Christ?*

3. *Why is self-sacrifice the greatest display of love? How was Judah's willingness to sacrifice himself for Benjamin a foreshadowing of what was to come in Christ?*

4. *How is a willingness to forgive related to an understanding of God's sovereignty? Is there anyone you need to forgive or seek reconciliation with today?*

5. *What promises of God can you cling to today? Can you be confident that He will keep His promises? Why or why not?*

JOURNAL

your thoughts

JOURNAL

your thoughts

6
5

"As for you, you meant to harm me, but God intended it for a good purpose, so he could preserve the lives of many people, as you can see this day."

Genesis 50:20

PRAY

Write down your prayer requests and praises for this week.

WEEKLY CHALLENGE

Jacob displayed great faith in God's promises even though he did not see them fully realized in his lifetime. This week, take time to find a few verses about God's promises for His people. Write them on a notecard and place them around your home to remind you of God's faithfulness and promise-keeping character.

WEEK 6
Monday

READ

Genesis 46:31—47:27

Then Joseph said to his brothers and his father's household, "I will go up and tell Pharaoh, 'My brothers and my father's household who were in the land of Canaan have come to me. 32 The men are shepherds; they take care of livestock. They have brought their flocks and their herds and all that they have.' 33 Pharaoh will summon you and say, 'What is your occupation?' 34 Tell him, 'Your servants have taken care of cattle from our youth until now, both we and our fathers,' so that you may live in the land of Goshen, for everyone who takes care of sheep is disgusting to the Egyptians." 47:1 Joseph went and told Pharaoh, "My father, my brothers, their flocks and herds, and all that they own have arrived from the land of Canaan. They are now in the land of Goshen." 2 He took five of his brothers and introduced them to Pharaoh. 3 Pharaoh said to Joseph's brothers, "What is your occupation?" They said to Pharaoh, "Your servants take care of flocks, just as our ancestors did." 4 Then they said to Pharaoh, "We have come to live as temporary residents in the land. There is no pasture for your servants' flocks because the famine is severe in the land of Canaan. So now, please let your servants live in the land of Goshen." 5 Pharaoh said to Joseph, "Your father and your brothers have come to you. 6 The land of Egypt is before you; settle your father and your brothers in the best region of the land. They may live in the land of Goshen. If you know of any highly capable men among them, put them in charge of my livestock." 7 Then Joseph brought in his father Jacob and presented him before Pharaoh. Jacob blessed Pharaoh. 8 Pharaoh said to Jacob, "How long have you lived?" 9 Jacob said to Pharaoh, "All the years of my travels are 130. All the years of my life have been few and painful; the years of my travels are not

WEEK 6
Monday

Genesis 46:31—47:27 (continued)

as long as those of my ancestors." 10 Then Jacob blessed
Pharaoh and went out from his presence. 11 So Joseph
settled his father and his brothers. He gave them territory
in the land of Egypt, in the best region of the land, the land
of Rameses, just as Pharaoh had commanded. 12 Joseph
also provided food for his father, his brothers, and all his
father's household, according to the number of their little
children. 13 But there was no food in all the land because
the famine was very severe; the land of Egypt and the land
of Canaan wasted away because of the famine. 14 Joseph
collected all the money that could be found in the land of
Egypt and in the land of Canaan as payment for the grain
they were buying. Then Joseph brought the money into
Pharaoh's palace. 15 When the money from the lands of
Egypt and Canaan was used up, all the Egyptians came to
Joseph and said, "Give us food! Why should we die before
your very eyes because our money has run out?" 16 Then
Joseph said, "If your money is gone, bring your livestock,
and I will give you food in exchange for your livestock."
17 So they brought their livestock to Joseph, and Joseph
gave them food in exchange for their horses, the livestock
of their flocks and herds, and their donkeys. He got them
through that year by giving them food in exchange for all
their livestock. 18 When that year was over, they came to
him the next year and said to him, "We cannot hide from
our lord that the money is used up and the livestock and
the animals belong to our lord. Nothing remains before our
lord except our bodies and our land. 19 Why should we die
before your very eyes, both we and our land? Buy us and
our land in exchange for food, and we, with our land, will
become Pharaoh's slaves. Give us seed that we may live and
not die. Then the land will not become desolate." 20 So
Joseph bought all the land of Egypt for Pharaoh. Each of

WEEK 6
Monday

Genesis 46:31—47:27 (continued)

the Egyptians sold his field, for the famine was severe. So
the land became Pharaoh's. 21 Joseph made all the people
slaves from one end of Egypt's border to the other end of it.
22 But he did not purchase the land of the priests because
the priests had an allotment from Pharaoh and they ate
from their allotment that Pharaoh gave them. That is why
they did not sell their land. 23 Joseph said to the people,
"Since I have bought you and your land today for Pharaoh,
here is seed for you. Cultivate the land. 24 When the crop
comes in, give one-fifth of it to Pharaoh. The remaining
four-fifths will be yours for seed for the fields and for you
to eat, including those in your households and your little
children." 25 They replied, "You have saved our lives! You
are showing us favor, and we will be Pharaoh's slaves."
26 So Joseph made it a statute, which is in effect to this
day throughout the land of Egypt: One-fifth belongs to
Pharaoh. Only the land of the priests did not become
Pharaoh's. 27 Israel settled in the land of Egypt, in the land
of Goshen, and they owned land there. They were fruitful
and increased rapidly in number.

Proverbs 8:12-17

"I, wisdom, have dwelt with prudence, and I find
knowledge and discretion. 13 The fear of the LORD is
to hate evil; I hate arrogant pride and the evil way and
perverse utterances. 14 Counsel and sound wisdom belong
to me; I possess understanding and might. 15 By me kings
reign, and by me potentates decree righteousness; 16 by
me princes rule, as well as nobles and all righteous judges.
17 I will love those who love me, and those who seek me
diligently will find me."

SOAP

WEEK 6 • MONDAY

SOAP / *Proverbs 8:15–17*

SCRIPTURE / *Write out the SOAP verses*

OBSERVATION / *Write 3 - 4 observations*

APPLICATION / *Write down 1 - 2 applications*

PRAYER / *Write out a prayer over what you learned*

SOAP

Proverbs 8:15–17

By me kings reign, and by me potentates decree righteousness; by me princes rule, as well as nobles and all righteous judges. I will love those who love me, and those who seek me diligently will find me.

INTO THE TEXT

As Jacob's family migrated to Egypt, Joseph gave his father and brothers specific instructions. They were to approach Pharaoh with honor and present themselves in the most favorable light. They showed great respect for Pharaoh and his authority, humbling themselves before him. Pharaoh showed them favor by giving them the best land in the region. Through this, Joseph was able to provide food for his family in a time of great famine.

As Pharaoh blessed Joseph and his family, Joseph blessed Pharaoh. Joseph saved many lives in a difficult situation. He permitted the people to sell their livestock, labor, and land to Pharaoh in exchange for food. Through this, Pharaoh became very wealthy. He prospered because he had blessed Jacob and his family, God's chosen people.

God ensured the survival of His chosen family through Joseph's wisdom. Throughout his life, Joseph continually chose the things of God, acting in wisdom beyond his years. Even from the earliest recorded action regarding his father's flocks, Joseph acted wisely. God used all of the circumstances in Joseph's life to develop wisdom in him, His chosen leader. While tending his father's flocks, managing Potiphar's house, interpreting dreams, and saving a nation and his own family from extinction, Joseph displayed wisdom. Joseph spent his life seeking wisdom from God, and, when it mattered most, the wisdom he gained helped him save many lives.

Joseph would be a model for kings and leaders to come. His leadership was an example to the nation of Israel of how to lead with God's wisdom. If God's chosen people were to survive, their leaders needed to serve and lead with great wisdom.

Today, Joseph's life still serves as an example for both those in positions of leadership and those submitting to their authority. Leaders must continually seek God's wisdom and allow Him to direct their steps. Similarly, as God's people, we must submit to the authorities God has appointed, whether national leaders like Pharaoh, or leaders in our local church. Those who lead with wisdom will indeed find blessing from God, and those who humble themselves before God's chosen leaders will find life and peace.

WEEK 6
Tuesday

READ

Genesis 47:28—48:22

Jacob lived in the land of Egypt seventeen years; the years of Jacob's life were 147 in all. 29 The time for Israel to die approached, so he called for his son Joseph and said to him, "If now I have found favor in your sight, put your hand under my thigh and show me kindness and faithfulness. Do not bury me in Egypt, 30 but when I rest with my fathers, carry me out of Egypt and bury me in their burial place." Joseph said, "I will do as you say." 31 Jacob said, "Swear to me that you will do so." So Joseph gave him his word. Then Israel bowed down at the head of his bed. 48:1 After these things Joseph was told, "Your father is weakening." So he took his two sons Manasseh and Ephraim with him. 2 When Jacob was told,"Your son Joseph has just come to you," Israel regained strength and sat up on his bed. 3 Jacob said to Joseph, "The Sovereign God appeared to me at Luz in the land of Canaan and blessed me. 4 He said to me, 'I am going to make you fruitful and will multiply you. I will make you into a group of nations, and I will give this land to your descendants as an everlasting possession.' 5 "Now, as for your two sons, who were born to you in the land of Egypt before I came to you in Egypt, they will be mine. Ephraim and Manasseh will be mine just as Reuben and Simeon are. 6 Any children that you father after them will be yours; they will be listed under the names of their brothers in their inheritance. 7 But as for me, when I was returning from Paddan, Rachel died—to my sorrow—in the land of Canaan. It happened along the way, some distance from Ephrath. So I buried her there on the way to Ephrath" (that is, Bethlehem). 8 When Israel saw Joseph's sons, he asked, "Who are these?" 9 Joseph said to his father, "They are the sons God has given me in this place." His father said, "Bring them to me so I may bless them." 10 Now Israel's

WEEK 6
Tuesday

Genesis 47:28—48:22 (continued)

eyes were failing because of his age; he was not able to
see well. So Joseph brought his sons near to him, and his
father kissed them and embraced them. 11 Israel said to
Joseph, "I never expected to see you again, but now God
has allowed me to see your children too." 12 So Joseph
moved them from Israel's knees and bowed down with his
face to the ground. 13 Joseph positioned them; he put
Ephraim on his right hand across from Israel's left hand,
and Manasseh on his left hand across from Israel's right
hand. Then Joseph brought them closer to his father.
14 Israel stretched out his right hand and placed it on
Ephraim's head, although he was the younger. Crossing
his hands, he put his left hand on Manasseh's head, for
Manasseh was the firstborn. 15 Then he blessed Joseph
and said, "May the God before whom my fathers Abraham
and Isaac walked— the God who has been my shepherd all
my life long to this day, 16 the angel who has protected
me from all harm— bless these boys. May my name be
named in them, and the name of my fathers Abraham and
Isaac. May they grow into a multitude on the earth." 17
When Joseph saw that his father placed his right hand on
Ephraim's head, it displeased him. So he took his father's
hand to move it from Ephraim's head to Manasseh's head.
18 Joseph said to his father, "Not so, my father, for this
is the firstborn. Put your right hand on his head." 19 But
his father refused and said, "I know, my son, I know. He
too will become a nation and he too will become great.
In spite of this, his younger brother will be even greater
and his descendants will become a multitude of nations."
20 So he blessed them that day, saying, "By you will
Israel bless, saying, 'May God make you like Ephraim

WEEK 6
Tuesday

Genesis 47:28—48:22 (continued)

and Manasseh.'" Thus he put Ephraim before Manasseh.
21 Then Israel said to Joseph, "I am about to die, but
God will be with you and will bring you back to the land
of your fathers. 22 As one who is above your brothers, I
give to you the mountain slope, which I took from the
Amorites with my sword and my bow."

Isaiah 55:8–9

"Indeed, my plans are not like your plans, and my deeds
are not like your deeds," says the Lord, 9 "for just as the
sky is higher than the earth, so my deeds are superior to
your deeds and my plans superior to your plans.

Philippians 1:6

For I am sure of this very thing, that the one who began a good work in you will perfect it until the day of Christ Jesus.

Hebrews 11:13

These all died in faith without receiving the things promised, but they saw them in the distance and welcomed them and acknowledged that they were strangers and foreigners on the earth.

Hebrews 11:21

By faith Jacob, as he was dying, blessed each of the sons of Joseph and ***worshiped as he leaned on his staff***.

SOAP

WEEK 6 • TUESDAY

SOAP / *Hebrews 11:13, 21*
SCRIPTURE / *Write out the SOAP verses*

OBSERVATION / *Write 3 - 4 observations*

APPLICATION / *Write down 1 - 2 applications*

PRAYER / *Write out a prayer over what you learned*

DEVOTIONAL

WEEK 6 • TUESDAY

SOAP

Hebrews 11:13, 21

These all died in faith without receiving the things promised, but they saw them in the distance and welcomed them and acknowledged that they were strangers and foreigners on the earth.

By faith Jacob, as he was dying, blessed each of the sons of Joseph and worshiped as he leaned on his staff.

INTO THE TEXT

Jacob's greatest act of faith came at the end of his life. He knew he was dying, and asked Joseph to promise to bury him in the land of his fathers, the land God promised to give to his descendants. When he blessed Ephraim, Joseph's second-born, as the firstborn, he displayed an understanding of the plans and purposes of God beyond his lifetime.

God's ways are not like ours. He is not bound by culture or ritual; He does as He pleases. Throughout the narrative of the patriarchs, God continually chose a younger son to inherit a blessing over the firstborn. In ancient Near Eastern culture, the firstborn received a blessing and a double portion of the inheritance from the father. However, God's choices depend on His eternal purposes, not birth order or cultural norms. Jacob understood this and did not question God's wisdom as he blessed Ephraim over Manasseh. He submitted to God's direction, acting in faith as he blessed the sons of Joseph.

Jacob's actions in this scene display God's continual work in his life. In previous events, Jacob acted deceitfully and out of self-reliance. He displayed passive tendencies and favoritism with his wives and sons. But God never stopped working in Jacob; He continually shaped him by His grace alone. After a lifetime of discipline, Jacob was able to discern the will of God. He had complete faith that God would continue to bless his family and bring them back to the land He promised to give them. Jacob learned to submit to the plan of God, and his family was blessed for it.

As our faith matures, we will become increasingly willing to submit to the plans and purposes of God. Jacob recognized that God's promise would not be fully realized in his lifetime, and he was confident that God would continue to be faithful to his family after his death. God never stopped working in Jacob, and He never stops working in us. He is continually shaping and molding us to be more like His Son, continually maturing us and disciplining us as He brings about His purposes. As we grow in our faith, we will become better able to discern the plans of God. We will become more willing to submit to His plan when it is different from ours. By acknowledging God's blessings to us in the past, we increase our faith in His ability and willingness to bless us in the future. He is always faithful, and He always keeps His promises.

WEEK 6
Wednesday

READ

Genesis 49:1–28

Jacob called for his sons and said, "Gather together so I can tell you what will happen to you in future days. 2 "Assemble and listen, you sons of Jacob; listen to Israel, your father. 3 Reuben, you are my firstborn, my might and the beginning of my strength, outstanding in dignity, outstanding in power. 4 You are destructive like water and will not excel, for you got on your father's bed, then you defiled it—he got on my couch! 5 Simeon and Levi are brothers, weapons of violence are their knives! 6 O my soul, do not come into their council, do not be united to their assembly, my heart, for in their anger they have killed men, and for pleasure they have hamstrung oxen. 7 Cursed be their anger, for it was fierce, and their fury, for it was cruel. I will divide them in Jacob, and scatter them in Israel! 8 Judah, your brothers will praise you. Your hand will be on the neck of your enemies, your father's sons will bow down before you. 9 You are a lion's cub, Judah, from the prey, my son, you have gone up. He crouches and lies down like a lion; like a lioness—who will rouse him? 10 The scepter will not depart from Judah, nor the ruler's staff from between his feet, until he comes to whom it belongs; the nations will obey him. 11 Binding his foal to the vine, and his colt to the choicest vine, he will wash his garments in wine, his robes in the blood of grapes. 12 His eyes will be red from wine, and his teeth white from milk. 13 Zebulun will live by the haven of the sea and become a haven for ships; his border will extend to Sidon. 14 Issachar is a strong-boned donkey lying down between two saddlebags. 15 When he sees a good resting place, and the pleasant land, he will bend his shoulder to the burden and become a slave laborer. 16 Dan will judge his people as one of the tribes of Israel. 17 May Dan be a snake beside the road, a viper by the path, that bites the heels of the horse so that its rider falls backward. 18 I wait for your deliverance, O Lord. 19 Gad will be raided by marauding bands, but he will attack them at their heels. 20 Asher's food will be rich, and he

WEEK 6
Wednesday

Genesis 49:1–28 (continued)

will provide delicacies to royalty. 21 Naphtali is a free running doe, he speaks delightful words. 22 Joseph is a fruitful bough, a fruitful bough near a spring whose branches climb over the wall. 23 The archers will attack him, they will shoot at him and oppose him. 24 But his bow will remain steady, and his hands will be skillful; because of the hands of the Powerful One of Jacob, because of the Shepherd, the Rock of Israel, 25 because of the God of your father, who will help you, because of the Sovereign God, who will bless you with blessings from the sky above, blessings from the deep that lies below, and blessings of the breasts and womb. 26 The blessings of your father are greater than the blessings of the eternal mountains or the desirable things of the age-old hills. They will be on the head of Joseph and on the brow of the prince of his brothers. 27 Benjamin is a ravenous wolf; in the morning devouring the prey, and in the evening dividing the plunder." 28 These are the twelve tribes of Israel. This is what their father said to them when he blessed them. He gave each of them an appropriate blessing.

Psalm 139:1–6

O Lord, you examine me and know me. 2 You know when I sit down and when I get up; even from far away you understand my motives. 3 You carefully observe me when I travel or when I lie down to rest; you are aware of everything I do. 4 Certainly my tongue does not frame a word without you, O Lord, being thoroughly aware of it. 5 You squeeze me in from behind and in front; you place your hand on me. 6 Your knowledge is beyond my comprehension; it is so far beyond me, I am unable to fathom it.

Psalm 139:16

Your eyes saw me when I was inside the womb. All the days ordained for me were recorded in your scroll before one of them came into existence.

God is sovereign and is always working out His good purposes for His kingdom, for His people, and for the world.

SOAP

WEEK 6 • WEDNESDAY

SOAP / *Psalm 139:16*

SCRIPTURE / *Write out the SOAP verses*

OBSERVATION / *Write 3 - 4 observations*

APPLICATION / *Write down 1 - 2 applications*

PRAYER / *Write out a prayer over what you learned*

SOAP

Psalm 139:16

Your eyes saw me when I was inside the womb. All the days ordained for me were recorded in your scroll before one of them came into existence.

INTO THE TEXT

In the final moments of Jacob's life, he spoke both blessing and prophecy over each of his sons. His words described the character of his sons, the blessings they would receive, and the characteristics and reputations of their descendants. Jacob displayed full confidence in God's plans for the future and full confidence in God's faithfulness to keep His promises. God had specific plans for each of Jacob's sons and their descendants, and, in His grace, He revealed some of those plans to Jacob.

For Reuben, Simeon, and Levi, their careless actions would keep them from receiving positions of leadership within the family and nation. While they would still receive blessing from God and carry the Abrahamic covenant forward, they would be disciplined for their actions. We can learn much from their example, seeing how sinful actions can often disqualify people from positions of leadership of God's people.

In contrast to the eldest three brothers, Judah and Joseph received great blessings and promises. Judah would be the father of the kings of Israel and Judah, the one through whom the Messiah would come. He would be the ancestor of the eternal King of Israel and the Messiah of the world, Jesus Christ.

Joseph received a double portion of blessing, as Jacob blessed Joseph's sons as his own. The faithfulness of Joseph allowed him to be blessed abundantly by God. In the same way that sinful actions can disqualify people from leadership, God entrusts these positions to those who are praiseworthy and responsible.

Even though these words were directed specifically to the sons and descendants of Jacob, we can find much encouragement and instruction in them. We are reminded of the way God knows our past, present, and future and of His intimate involvement in each.

God has specific plans and a specific future designed for each of us. Will we submit our lives, desires, and plans to God, trusting He has the perfect future prepared for us? As we seek to live lives that honor Him, may we begin each day by entrusting our future to the One who has known all our days before any of them came to be.

WEEK 6
Thursday

READ

Genesis 49:29—50:26

Then he instructed them, "I am about to go to my people.
Bury me with my fathers in the cave in the field of Ephron
the Hittite. 30 It is the cave in the field of Machpelah,
near Mamre in the land of Canaan, which Abraham bought
for a burial plot from Ephron the Hittite. 31 There they
buried Abraham and his wife Sarah; there they buried Isaac
and his wife Rebekah; and there I buried Leah. 32 The
field and the cave in it were acquired from the sons of
Heth." 33 When Jacob finished giving these instructions
to his sons, he pulled his feet up onto the bed, breathed
his last breath, and went to his people. 50:1 Then Joseph
hugged his father's face. He wept over him and kissed him.
2 Joseph instructed the physicians in his service to embalm
his father, so the physicians embalmed Israel. 3 They took
forty days, for that is the full time needed for embalming.
The Egyptians mourned for him seventy days. 4 When the
days of mourning had passed, Joseph said to Pharaoh's royal
court, "If I have found favor in your sight, please say to
Pharaoh, 5 'My father made me swear an oath. He said, "I
am about to die. Bury me in my tomb that I dug for myself
there in the land of Canaan." Now let me go and bury my
father; then I will return.'" 6 So Pharaoh said, "Go and
bury your father, just as he made you swear to do." 7 So
Joseph went up to bury his father; all Pharaoh's officials
went with him—the senior courtiers of his household,
all the senior officials of the land of Egypt, 8 all Joseph's
household, his brothers, and his father's household. But
they left their little children and their flocks and herds in
the land of Goshen. 9 Chariots and horsemen also went
up with him, so it was a very large entourage. 10 When
they came to the threshing floor of Atad on the other side
of the Jordan, they mourned there with very great and

WEEK 6
Thursday

Genesis 49:29—50:26 (continued)

bitter sorrow. There Joseph observed a seven-day period
of mourning for his father. 11 When the Canaanites who
lived in the land saw them mourning at the threshing floor
of Atad, they said, "This is a very sad occasion for the
Egyptians." That is why its name was called Abel Mizraim,
which is beyond the Jordan. 12 So the sons of Jacob did for
him just as he had instructed them. 13 His sons carried him
to the land of Canaan and buried him in the cave of the
field of Machpelah, near Mamre. This is the field Abraham
purchased as a burial plot from Ephron the Hittite. 14
After he buried his father, Joseph returned to Egypt, along
with his brothers and all who had accompanied him to
bury his father. 15 When Joseph's brothers saw that their
father was dead, they said, "What if Joseph bears a grudge
and wants to repay us in full for all the harm we did to
him?" 16 So they sent word to Joseph, saying, "Your father
gave these instructions before he died: 17 'Tell Joseph this:
Please forgive the sin of your brothers and the wrong they
did when they treated you so badly.' Now please forgive the
sin of the servants of the God of your father." When this
message was reported to him, Joseph wept. 18 Then his
brothers also came and threw themselves down before him;
they said, "Here we are; we are your slaves." 19 But Joseph
answered them, "Don't be afraid. Am I in the place of God?
20 As for you, you meant to harm me, but God intended it
for a good purpose, so he could preserve the lives of many
people, as you can see this day. 21 So now, don't be afraid.
I will provide for you and your little children." Then he

WEEK 6
Thursday

Genesis 49:29—50:26 (continued)

consoled them and spoke kindly to them. 22 Joseph lived in Egypt, along with his father's family. Joseph lived 110 years. 23 Joseph saw the descendants of Ephraim to the third generation. He also saw the children of Makir the son of Manasseh; they were given special inheritance rights by Joseph. 24 Then Joseph said to his brothers, "I am about to die. But God will surely come to you and lead you up from this land to the land he swore on oath to give to Abraham, Isaac, and Jacob." 25 Joseph made the sons of Israel swear an oath. He said, "God will surely come to you. Then you must carry my bones up from this place." 26 So Joseph died at the age of 110. After they embalmed him, his body was placed in a coffin in Egypt.

Exodus 13:19

Moses took the bones of Joseph with him, for Joseph had made the Israelites solemnly swear, "God will surely attend to you, and you will carry my bones up from this place with you."

John 14:1–3

"Do not let your hearts be distressed. You believe in God; believe also in me. 2 There are many dwelling places in my Father's house. Otherwise, I would have told you, because I am going away to make ready a place for you. 3 And if I go and make ready a place for you, I will come again and take you to be with me, so that where I am you may be too.

SOAP

WEEK 6 • THURSDAY

SOAP / *John 14:1–3*

SCRIPTURE / *Write out the SOAP verses*

OBSERVATION / *Write 3 - 4 observations*

APPLICATION / *Write down 1 - 2 applications*

PRAYER / *Write out a prayer over what you learned*

SOAP

John 14:1–3

"Do not let your hearts be distressed. You believe in God; believe also in me. There are many dwelling places in my Father's house. Otherwise, I would have told you, because I am going away to make a place ready for you. And if I go and make ready a place for you, I will come again and take you to be with me, so that where I am you may be too."

INTO THE TEXT

The final chapter of Genesis brings the events of both Jacob's and Joseph's lives to a close. Both men showed great faith in God's promises in their final days. They knew Egypt was not their home. God promised to give them a land of their own, and Egypt was not it. While neither Jacob nor Joseph saw God fulfill that promise, they both acted in faith by instructing their sons to bring their bones back to the land of promise.

Jacob and Joseph lived in anticipation of the long-awaited blessing of God. They were convinced God would deliver His people to the land He promised to give them. After his death, Jacob's sons and his entire household carried his body to the burial plot Abraham purchased from the Hittite. Jacob was buried with his fathers, resting in the land of promise. This procession foreshadowed another one to come years later when Moses brought the bones of Joseph out of Egypt and the Israelites were freed from slavery. Both men displayed their faith in God's promise even though they did not see the promise completed.

Believers in Christ today are also waiting for the fulfillment of a great promise. Jesus has promised to return and to give all His followers a final resting place with Him. He has prepared a place for all who believe in Him and have accepted Him as their Lord and Savior. Today, as believers in Christ, we are longing for the fulfillment of that promise.

The death of a believer in Christ is not the end. Instead, it is the beginning of the full realization of all the wonderful promises of God. Jacob and Joseph died believing God would fulfill His promise and bring their descendants to His promised land. Similarly, when believers in Christ die, they do so believing that God will fulfill His promise, taking them with Him to the place He has promised, the place He has prepared for them. When we live and die based on God's promises, death loses its power. For nothing can keep us from inheriting the promises of God, not even death.

WEEK 6
Friday

READ

Genesis 1:31

God saw all that he had made—and it was very good! There was evening, and there was morning, the sixth day.

Genesis 3:4–6

The serpent said to the woman, "Surely you will not die, 5 for God knows that when you eat from it your eyes will open and you will be like God, knowing good and evil." 6 When the woman saw that the tree produced fruit that was good for food,was attractive to the eye, and was desirable for making one wise, she took some of its fruit and ate it. She also gave some of it to her husband who was with her, and he ate it.

Genesis 6:5–8

But the LORD saw that the wickedness of humankind had become great on the earth. Every inclination of the thoughts of their minds was only evil all the time. 6 The LORD regretted that he had made humankind on the earth, and he was highly offended. 7 So the LORD said, "I will wipe humankind, whom I have created, from the face of the earth—everything from humankind to animals, including creatures that move on the ground and birds of the air, for I regret that I have made them." 8 But Noah found favor in the sight of the LORD.

WEEK 6
Friday

Genesis 18:22–25

The two men turned and headed toward Sodom, but
Abraham was still standing before the Lord. 23 Abraham
approached and said, "Will you really sweep away the godly
along with the wicked? 24 What if there are fifty godly
people in the city? Will you really wipe it out and not spare
the place for the sake of the fifty godly people who are in it?
25 Far be it from you to do such a thing—to kill the godly
with the wicked, treating the godly and the wicked alike!
Far be it from you! Will not the judge of the whole earth
do what is right?"

Genesis 50:19–20

But Joseph answered them, "Don't be afraid. Am I in the
place of God? 20 As for you, you meant to harm me, but
God intended it for a good purpose, so he could preserve
the lives of many people, as you can see this day.

May we recognize God's mercy, provision, and grace in all things.

SOAP

WEEK 6 • FRIDAY

SOAP / *Genesis 50:19–20*

SCRIPTURE / *Write out the SOAP verses*

OBSERVATION / *Write 3 - 4 observations*

APPLICATION / *Write down 1 - 2 applications*

PRAYER / *Write out a prayer over what you learned*

DEVOTIONAL

WEEK 6 • FRIDAY

SOAP

Genesis 50:19–20

But Joseph answered them, "Don't be afraid. Am I in the place of God? As for you, you meant to harm me, but God intended it for a good purpose, so he could preserve the lives of many people, as you can see this day."

INTO THE TEXT

One of the main themes of the Book of Genesis is the theme of good versus evil. Throughout the book, the author provides examples of good, examples of evil, and the interaction between the two. Beginning with the creation account and continuing to the story of Joseph, the author displays God's sovereignty through this theme.

God created the heavens and the earth. After He completed His work, God called all that He made good. Evil had not yet entered the world. God placed the man and the woman He created in an orchard, allowing them to eat from whatever tree they desired, except for two. The serpent tricked them, promising the woman that if she ate from the tree of the knowledge of good and evil, she would be like God, knowing good and evil. She and the man both ate, and they were suddenly aware of evil because they had committed the first act of sin.

Later, God declared that all the thoughts and actions of human beings were only evil all the time. He promised to destroy all He had made because of this great wickedness. Yet even in the midst of such evil, there was one man who found favor with God.

Much later, God chose a man named Abraham to be the one through whom God would keep His promise to redeem the world from evil and sin. Abraham knew God was righteous and good. God would not destroy the good along with the wicked, but would instead allow evil to prevail to save those who were committed to Him.

In Joseph's life, God used a great evil to bring about a great good. His brothers had thrown him into a well and sold him into slavery. He was persecuted and falsely accused, thrown into prison without a trial. Even in all this evil, God would bring about His good purpose. Joseph not only allowed God to direct his steps and use his life for His purposes, but He recognized the sovereignty of God in bringing about good from intended harm.

God's sovereignty remains unchanged. While it may often seem that evil is triumphant in the world, God is always bringing about His good purposes. Nothing is beyond His reach. Nothing goes unnoticed by Him. As we endure an evil world, we can be confident that no matter the circumstances, God is sovereign and is always working out His good purposes for His kingdom, for His people, and for the world.

REFLECT

WEEK 6

1. *Why is it important for God's leaders to have wisdom? How can you lead with wisdom today? How can you also humble yourself and submit to the authorities God has placed in your life?*

....

....

....

2. *In what area of your life is it easiest for you to trust God? In what area of your life is it most difficult for you to trust God? Why is it necessary to submit to God's plans when they are different from yours?*

....

....

....

3. *What is your reaction to hearing that God knew all of your days before one of them came to be?*

....

....

....

4. *Have you accepted Christ as your Lord and Savior? If so, do you believe He is preparing a place for you? How can you live in light of this marvelous promise?*

....

....

....

5. *In what ways have you seen God turn something intended by others to harm you into something good?*

....

....

....

JOURNAL

your thoughts

JOURNAL

your thoughts

Bri

BRIDGE

SOAP it up between studies
2 week reading plan

Have you developed a consistent, daily Bible study habit and don't want to break it before our next study begins? You can study along with our 2 week Bridge Reading Plan and continue your growth using the SOAP method. For more materials (including the *Love God Greatly SOAP Journal*), blogs, and Bible studies, you can visit lovegodgreatly.com.

READING PLAN

WEEK 1

○ *Monday*
Read: Proverbs 17:15–28
SOAP: Proverbs 17:27–28

○ *Tuesday*
Read: Proverbs 18:1–12
SOAP: Proverbs 18:10

○ *Wednesday*
Read: Proverbs 18:13–24
SOAP: Proverbs 18:16

○ *Thursday*
Read: Proverbs 19:1–10
SOAP: Proverbs 19:5

○ *Friday*
Read: Proverbs 19:11–19
SOAP: Proverbs 19:11

WEEK 2

○ *Monday*
Read: Proverbs 19:20–29
SOAP: Proverbs 19:23

○ *Tuesday*
Read: Proverbs 20:1–15
SOAP: Proverbs 20:11

○ *Wednesday*
Read: Proverbs 20:16–30
SOAP: Proverbs 20:22

○ *Thursday*
Read: Proverbs 21:1–15
SOAP: Proverbs 21:2–3

○ *Friday*
Read: Proverbs 21:16–31
SOAP: Proverbs 21:25–26

Join Us

ONLINE
lovegodgreatly.com

SHOP
lovegodgreatly.com

FACEBOOK
Love God Greatly

INSTAGRAM
@lovegodgreatlyofficial

APP
Love God Greatly

CONTACT US
info@lovegodgreatly.com

CONNECT
#LoveGodGreatly

FOR YOU

What we offer

40+ Translations	Love God Greatly Journal
Bible Reading Plans	Bible Study Journals
Online Bible Study	Community Groups
Love God Greatly App	Love God Greatly Bible
Over 200 Countries Served	Young Women Love God Greatly Bible

Each study includes

Three Weekly Blog Posts	Weekly Challenges
Daily Devotions	Weekly Reflection Questions
Memory Verses	Bridge Reading Plan

Other studies

Beautifully Surrendered	Love the Loveless
Our Security for Eternity	Truth Over Lies
The Importance of Prayer	1 & 2 Thessalonians
The Greatest Gift Given	Fear & Anxiety
In Jesus You Are...	James
Friendship	His Name Is...
In the Beginning	Philippians
The Gospel of Mark	1 & 2 Timothy
Shame Breaker	Sold Out
Everlasting Covenant	Ruth
Jesus Our Everything	Broken & Redeemed
Know Love	Walking in Wisdom
Empowered: Yesterday and Today	God With Us
Risen	In Everything Give Thanks
Draw Near	You Are Forgiven
Beatitudes	David
Esther	Ecclesiastes
Words Matter	Names of God
Walking in Victory	Galatians
To Do Justice, To Love Kindness, To Walk Humbly	Psalm 119
	1st & 2nd Peter
Faithful Love	Made For Community
Choose Brave	The Road To Christmas
Savior	The Source Of Gratitude
Promises of God	You Are Loved